Container Gardening *for the* Midwest

William Aldrich and Don Williamson

with Alison Beck and Laura Peters

LONE PINE

Lone Pine Publishing International

The Distributor: Lone Pine Publishing
1808 B Street, Suite 140
Auburn, WA USA 98001
Website: www.lonepinepublishing.com

Publisher's Cataloging-In-Publication Data
(Prepared by The Donohue Group, Inc.)

Aldrich, William, 1948-
    Container gardening for the Midwest / William Aldrich and Don Williamson ; with Alison Beck and Laura Peters.

    p. : ill. ; cm.

    Includes index.
    ISBN-13: 978-976-8200-42-6
    ISBN-10: 976-8200-42-1

    1. Container gardening--Middle West. I. Williamson, Don, 1962- II. Beck, Alison. III. Peters, Laura, 1968- IV. Title.

SB418 .A43 2008
635.9/860977

Front cover photograph by Proven Winners

All photos by Laura Peters except;
AA Selection 154b, 159b; Ball Horticultural Co. 144; Sandra Bit 137b; Tamara Eder 74, 85, 92, 96, 110a, 110b, 115, 117b, 120, 121a, 127a, 138b, 143b, 151, 161, 165b, 166a, 166b, 170b, 188, 192a, 194c; Derek Fell 65, 78, 79b, 135; Erika Flatt 84; Saxon Holt 141; Liz Klose 135, 141; Janet Loughrey 171; Heather Markham 125a; Tim Matheson 67a, 75b, 99, 100, 107a, 108a, 111, 117a, 123b, 124, 125b, 127b, 130, 138a, 143a, 143c, 149, 175, 176, 190, 191c, 194a, 194b; Marilyn McAra 186b; Kim O'Leary 86a, Allison Penko 117a, 127b; Proven Winners 64, 66, 69, 80, 88, 90a, 91, 93, 97, 98, 101a, 101b, 104a, 104b, 106, 107b, 108b, 116, 118, 122, 131, 133, 146, 148, 152, 156, 162, 163, 168, 169, 172, 173a, 180, 182, 183, 187, 189; Nanette Samol 191a, 191b; Peter Thompstone 145; Vincent Woo 13; Tim Wood 67b, 102a, 102b, 102c, 192b.

PC:*P15*

Table of Contents

Preface

There is a wonderful day each spring when a line of containers and an array of colorful nursery plants meet and decisions must be made as to what goes where. Mixing and matching, wrestling with potting mix, slow-release fertilizer, a water source—it all sounds like work until you think back to the long Midwest winter and how much you've missed this type of creativity. Once completed, the pots look almost scrawny with their fresh new transplants, but the optimistic gardener realizes that with a little luck and consistent watering, these combinations will grow and knit into wonderful gardens unto themselves.

Container gardening is the fastest growing segment of the American gardening scene, with great justification. Wonderful new pots continue to make their appearance each spring at garden centers in materials that range from opulent fired clays to light-weight resins. "Outdoor living" is the watchword, bringing new definitions to patios and decks—and with it, new spaces for creative planters. Breeders continue to bring us new and unusual plant varieties, many in unique foliage textures that ache to find a home in a window box or hanging basket.

Throughout the book, we will try to alert you as to whether the plant is easy, a bit of a challenge or somewhat difficult to grow. These alerts are aimed more at a newer gardener who has not tried a particular species; veteran gardeners will know most of the cultural nuances and won't be fazed by a more difficult rating.

We will also try to alert you as to the type of growth you can expect based on three principles of container design: thrillers, spillers and fillers. Thrillers are the knock-out elements of the combination planter, whether in height or overall size. Think of a spike (*Dracaena*) in the center of an arrangement, but of course we want to steer you to something with more punch. Spillers are that wonderful class of plant that cascades over the pot rim and adds a third spatial dimension. Think sweet potato vine. Fillers are the plants that sprawl through a pot, typically lower than the tallest element. Think petunias or coleus.

Once the spring flurry is gone, don't think you can't put together another container garden. Make one for fall in late summer, or take a trip to the store in early winter and bring home succulents for an indoor dish garden; the list goes on and on. It's easy. It's fun. Let the creative juices flow.

~William Aldrich

The Plants at a Glance

Pictorial Guide in Alphabetical Order

African Daisy
p. 64

Alternanthera
p. 65

Arborvitae
p. 66

Asparagus Fern
p. 68

Bacopa
p. 69

Banana
p. 70

Basil
p. 71

Black-Eyed Susan
p. 74

Black-Eyed Susan Vine
p. 76

Begonia
p. 72

Blood Grass
p. 77

Blueberry
p. 78

Blue Fescue
p. 80

Caladium
p. 81

Calla Lily
p. 82

Canna Lily
p. 84

Clematis
p. 85

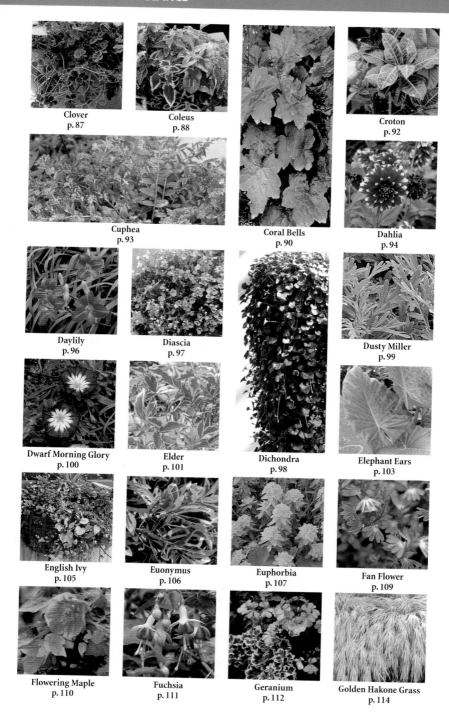

Clover
p. 87

Coleus
p. 88

Croton
p. 92

Cuphea
p. 93

Coral Bells
p. 90

Dahlia
p. 94

Daylily
p. 96

Diascia
p. 97

Dusty Miller
p. 99

Dwarf Morning Glory
p. 100

Elder
p. 101

Dichondra
p. 98

Elephant Ears
p. 103

English Ivy
p. 105

Euonymus
p. 106

Euphorbia
p. 107

Fan Flower
p. 109

Flowering Maple
p. 110

Fuchsia
p. 111

Geranium
p. 112

Golden Hakone Grass
p. 114

Golden Marguerite
p. 115

Heliotrope
p. 118

Hens and Chicks
p. 119

Hardy Geranium
p. 116

Hosta
p. 120

Impatiens
p. 124

Iris
p. 126

Japanese Painted Fern
p. 128

Hydrangea
p. 122

Lady's Mantle
p. 130

Lamium
p. 131

Lantana
p. 133

Lavender
p. 134

Lemon
p. 135

Licorice Plant
p. 136

Lobelia
p. 137

Lotus Vine
p. 139

Maidenhair Fern
p. 140

Mandevilla
p. 141

Maple
p. 142

Maracas Brazilian
Fireworks p. 144

Million Bells
p. 145

Mondo Grass
p. 146

Nasturtium
p. 147

Nemesia
p. 148

Nicotiana
p. 149

Oregano
p. 150

Ornamental Pepper
p. 151

Oxalis
p. 152

Pansy
p. 153

Parsley
p. 155

Perilla
p. 156

Periwinkle
p. 157

Petunia
p. 158

Piggyback Plant
p. 161

Plectranthus
p. 162

Phormium
p. 160

Rose
p. 165

Purple Fountain Grass
p. 163

Rosemary
p. 167

Rush
p. 168

Salvia
p. 169

Scarlet Runner Bean
p. 171

Sedge
p. 172

Sedum
p. 174

Spider Flower
p. 176

Spider Plant
p. 177

Spike
p. 178

Snapdragon
p. 175

Spruce
p. 179

Swan River Daisy
p. 180

Sweet Alyssum
p. 181

Sweet Flag
p. 182

Sweet Potato Vine
p. 183

Thyme
p. 185

Tropical Hibiscus
p. 186

Verbena
p. 187

Vinca
p. 188

Weigela
p. 189

Yarrow
p. 190

Yew
p. 192

Yucca
p. 193

Introduction

Many people tend to see gardens as more work than they're worth, especially when, after an investment of time and effort, they still somehow don't measure up to our perception of beauty. On the flip side, many other people don't have access to a plot of land, and thereby allege they can't garden because there is only a balcony, patio or shared common area that is managed by a professional service provider. Enter the container and the entire field of container gardening. Almost every plant that can be grown in a conventional garden can be grown on a smaller scale in a container.

A well-designed container or grouping of containers can look stunning with trailing plants cascading over the edges and colorful mounds of delicate flowers and interesting foliage filling the centers. You can use containers to create theme gardens, grow vegetables, plant an orchard or grow flowers for a vase or herbs to add to favorite recipes. A small deck or patio can be transformed into a tropical oasis, an English cottage garden or a shaded woodland when pots of different shapes and sizes are filled with varied plant combinations to achieve a certain feel, look or environment. Gardening in all its incarnations should be fun and enjoyable, and container gardening is no exception. Even one large container can provide you with all the pleasure gardening has to offer.

Container gardening can be a benefit to people with limited mobility, such as the disabled and the elderly, who require easy accessibility to their gardens. A garden with wide paths, raised beds and containers is ideal for able-bodied gardeners but even better for those who require the extra space for accessibility and stability. A stable, wide edge of a raised bed offers a seating area at a comfortable height for people who cannot work for extended periods while standing.

Container gardening is a wonderful way to enhance larger gardens and landscapes. Containers expand the space available for growing plants, especially those plants that require specific growing conditions such as soil that is not typical for the area. Many containers can be easily moved to take advantage of light conditions not available in the regular planting areas of your garden or landscape. Containers with more tender plants can be moved to areas where they will be protected from the elements. Using containers as a physical barrier to confine plants with invasive tendencies allows you to grow these plants without having to contend with their spreading into unwanted places.

Container plants are used as focal points, set in places to draw your attention or to mark entrances such as doorways,

sidewalks, driveways and garden paths. Beautifully planted containers can be used to draw your eyes away from distracting items or areas you would prefer to remain unnoticed. Containers can also be placed in beds and borders to fill gaps left by plants that finished blooming earlier in the season, were decimated by pests or disease or were simply not performing as desired.

Containers are also great places to experiment with companion planting. Companion plants are those that form a symbiotic relationship when planted together, such as one plant providing protection from pests while the other plant provides nutrients needed by the first.

Container gardening can be a time and money saver. Many of the tedious chores such as weeding, mowing, digging and raking are reduced or eliminated when you garden in containers. The use of automated watering systems or water-holding polymers and other materials, combined with slow-release fertilizers, can make your container garden a very low-maintenance affair. The smaller gardening area will also cost less than an average garden. You will have to make an initial investment in containers and a few tools and supplies, but your annual costs will include only plants, fertilizer and growing media.

The only limits to what can be done with container gardening are the limits you place on yourself. There is really no way to fail at gardening if you keep an open mind. That's the beauty of container gardening—there's no long-term commitment. You can change your containers completely from one season to the next, regardless of what you've chosen to grow, and experiment with combinations of plants until you discover the perfect arrangement.

Vertical and Rooftop Gardening

Vertical Gardening

Vertical gardening makes the most of a limited space, such as a balcony or patio. Vertical gardens can be used to block an ugly view or to provide privacy. Vertical gardening also allows the disabled and elderly easier access for maintaining the plants and enjoying the garden.

Vertical gardening is as easy to do in containers as it is in a regular garden. Containers that can be used for vertical gardening include raised beds, planter boxes and hanging baskets.

Vines and other natural climbers can be trained to grow up trellises, fences, arbors and walls, using space that would otherwise remain empty. Some vines will naturally twine around a structure, some will attach themselves to the structure with tendrils, aerial rootlets or suction cups, and some plants need to be attached to the structure with soft ties. You will need to ensure that the container and climbing structure are sturdy enough to handle the weight without tipping over and that they will not blow over in a strong wind.

Plants can be grown in hanging baskets and allowed to trail and spill over the edges of the baskets. Hanging baskets can be hung from any sturdy support, ranging from commercially available poles to house eaves to tree branches.

Hanging baskets can be raised and lowered with a pulley system, which makes maintaining the baskets easier. A small block and tackle system allows for heavy containers to be raised and lowered with ease. Tie a knot in the pulley rope so that if the rope slips out of your hands, the container will not hit the ground. Ladders can be used to reach higher baskets if a pulley system is not possible. Watering can be done with a hose-end watering wand designed to reach up and into hanging baskets.

If you are going to hang a basket from a tree branch, make sure the strap is wide enough that the branch is not damaged and that the branch is strong enough to support the weight of the basket.

Plants can also be grown in a variety of specialized containers including multiple-opening containers, stackable containers and grow walls. We are all familiar with the terra-cotta strawberry/herb planter that has a large opening at the top and smaller openings around the sides. There are now many styles of commercially available containers with multiple openings. There are stackable containers that allow far more plants to be grown in a small surface area than do regular containers and in-ground gardens. Growing walls are containers that have a vertical planting surface. One type of growing wall is a tall, flat, upright container that resembles a section of lattice fence with plants poking out of it. Another type is a wall constructed of custom-formed cinder blocks that provide planting pockets at regular intervals. A growing wall can stand alone or be incorporated as part of a building wall, fence or barrier. There are also retaining wall blocks that have preformed planting pockets in the design, so your whole retaining wall can be planted.

Some pest problems experienced in regular gardens are reduced or eliminated in a containerized vertical garden. Hanging baskets and upside-down containers prevent crawling pests from reaching the plants, and the plants are more exposed to the air, which reduces the incidence of many diseases.

Your vertical container garden requires the same type of maintenance as a regular container garden, except the plants may need to be watered more frequently. A layer of mulch will help retain moisture. You will need to determine if your vertical garden will be shading other plants, and keep in mind that the amount of shade will increase as the season progresses. Try to grow plants that will remain in easy reach for maintenance. If you are growing sun-loving plants, place the climbing structure on the north side of the plants. Do the reverse for shade-loving plants. Also, be aware of the direction of the prevailing wind, and face the plants into the wind so that it pushes the plants onto the structure.

Rooftop Gardening

Rooftop gardening is one of the latest "hot" trends in horticulture. Rooftop gardens come in different forms, from a thick layer of soil over an impermeable membrane that covers most of the roof surface to a collection of various containers merely set on the roof. Rooftop gardens reduce pest problems even further than on-the-ground container gardens, as any pest that has to crawl or

walk to find its host, such as a browsing deer, is out of luck. Vandalism and theft are reduced as well. Rooftop gardens in large urban centers provide respite for birds and butterflies that might otherwise lack adequate food and shelter.

Container gardening is ideal for a rooftop, but you must make sure the structure is sturdy enough to handle the weight of pots, plants, soil and water. A structural engineer will be needed to determine how much weight your roof can hold. You may be able to

have your containers on the roof in spring, summer and fall but will need to remove them if you get any appreciable snow cover in winter. The roof might not take the weight of the containers and snow combined.

You will need to have a handy source of water for the plants. Be aware that there will be more sunlight and wind on the rooftop, and containers will need to be watered every day. You can incorporate water-holding polymers into the potting soil and mulches to keep the containers moist. It is a good idea to trap as much rainwater for use as possible. You do not want to be hauling buckets of water up to the roof just to water the plants. Pots, plants, soil, etc., will also need to be transported to the rooftop.

Much as you might want to start a rooftop garden, access may be limited. There might be restrictions as to who is allowed on the roof if it is a commercial building or apartment. Some municipalities require railings around the edge of the building to prevent falling.

Rooftop gardens extend the growing season because rooftops tend to be a warmer and drier microclimate. However, winds at rooftop level can be strong and can break trees and shred herbaceous plants. Sturdy windbreaks can protect the plants from strong winds. Windbreaks will also provide some shade from intense afternoon sun and some privacy from neighbors. You will need to provide extra protection for evergreen plants in containers in winter because the wind and sun can quickly desiccate a plant. Some plants may be better adapted to rooftop culture than others. Heat-loving plants such as hens and chicks, moss rose and herbs are drought tolerant and are excellent choices for the rooftop.

Container Design

Choosing what you like from what will grow well in the conditions of your growing space is one of the steps to planning any garden. Deciding how to combine these plants is another important step. Containers should be treated like small flowerbeds, and the same principles of design apply as with ground-based plantings. There are no hard and fast rules to container design, but the following suggestions may help to determine what will grow successfully and what will appeal to the eye.

Thrillers, spillers and fillers: include a variety of flower shapes and at least three different foliage textures. Overall container garden designs look best with at least one strong, vertical element (the thriller), colorful mid-level plants (the fillers) and one or more plants draping over the edge of the pot or basket (the spillers).

Combining several different types of plants together (above, below & bottom right).

Group plants that have the same needs together, such as water-loving plants, shade-tolerant plants or drought-resistant plants. This will make it simpler to take care of each container and can help prevent problems with insects and diseases.

If you combine several types of plants in one container, generally keep the tallest ones in the middle or, if the container will be against a wall, fence or railing, to the back of the container. Compact and trailing plants can be kept closer to the front or the edge of the container so that they are not lost visually. Some of the more robust trailing plants are good choices for the corners of square containers, where they have some extra room to spread. Careful planning allows for the best light to reach all plants, makes them all easy to see and enjoy and gives the containers an attractive, well-balanced appearance.

You can use tall, sun-loving plants to provide shade for other plants. A trellis covered with tall, fast-growing morning glories, scarlet runner beans or hops will shade a container of impatiens or hostas.

Color

Color is often the first thing we notice in a garden. It is easy to make a dramatic statement with color in containers and container gardens because they are confined and right in front of you. Traditional ground-based gardens take more effort to create those dramatic effects.

Sometimes, knowing where to start is overwhelming. Take inspiration from home decorating and lifestyle magazines or anything that inspires you. Keep in mind that different colors have different effects on our senses.

Cool colors, such as blue, purple and green, are soothing and can make small spaces seem bigger.

Warm colors, such as red, orange and yellow, are more stimulating and appear to fill large spaces.

White combines well with any color, and plants that bloom in white help to keep the garden from becoming a blurry, tangled mess.

People use color in their homes to relax. This formula can also be used outdoors, especially in small spaces. Green combinations can provide a refreshing feel to a space, while pinks and blues can invoke a romantic environment. Fiery yellows, oranges and reds will add a liveliness and warmth to even the largest, most imposing spaces, and bronze, brown and neutral tones can appear contemporary and classy.

There are a couple of aspects of color to be aware of when planning your containers: color echoing and color harmonies. Color echoing involves repeating one color, which can be of various hues

PROVEN WINNERS

Cool colors (above) are soothing. Color echoing with warm colors (below).

and intensities, throughout the garden to produce unity and flow. This has the effect of making it easy for your eyes to move from one part of the garden to the next without abrupt changes. It is wise to keep the color of your house, outbuildings and structures such as fences in mind when deciding what color or colors to use.

Color harmonies involve the color designs we use to plan our containers, and they are easy to understand with the use of a color wheel.

Monochromatic designs use one color that varies in hue and intensity or other colors very close to it on the color wheel. For example, a monochromatic planting of yellow may include yellow-green without disturbing the harmony of the planting.

Using black and white in the garden.

PROVEN WINNERS

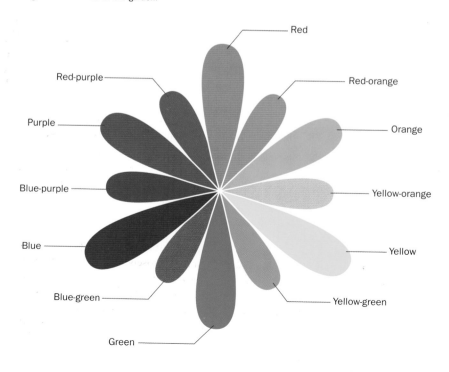

Red

Red-purple

Red-orange

Purple

Orange

Blue-purple

Yellow-orange

Blue

Yellow

Blue-green

Yellow-green

Green

Analogous (above). Polychromatic (below).   Monochromatic (above). Complementary (below).

Analogous color designs use colors that are next to each other on the wheel, such as using blues with violets and greens. These colors add more spice to a design while maintaining the same mood of the planting.

Complementary color designs use colors that are opposite on the color wheel. These combinations make bold and dramatic plantings that are hard to ignore.

Neutral colors, the near-blacks of some foliage plants or white and gray/silver,

make other colors stand out, add depth to smaller areas and plantings and help tone down strong and complementary colors. A planting with all white flowers is a good choice for people whose gardening time is limited to twilight and evening hours.

Polychromatic color designs are those that most closely resemble the designs done by Mother Nature—a mixture of colors and textures seemingly tossed together in a haphazard manner. These can be some of the easiest designs to do.

PROVEN WINNERS

Texture

Texture is an important consideration in container planting, affecting the perception of a container's size and space.

Foliage is the key to varying textures. Large leaves are considered coarsely textured. Their visibility from a greater distance makes spaces seem smaller and more shaded. Small leaves, or those that are finely divided, are considered finely textured and create a sense of greater space and light.

Textures, colors and size of foliage can vary greatly, creating a myriad of combinations. Integrating textural diversity into a container encourages people to get up close to touch the leaves. You'll want to determine whether foliage is rough, soft, spiky or smooth. Flowers come and go, but a container garden planned with careful attention to foliage, using a mix of coarse, medium and fine textures, will always be interesting.

Scale and Proportion

The scale and proportion of plants should match the size of the containers you plan to use. For container designs featuring a tall focal plant, the finished height should ideally be one to one-and-a-half times the height of the container. The exception to these guidelines would be for large specimen plants, which demand their own container, or at most have a fringe of trailing plants, and often exceed the suggested plant-to-container height ratio.

The scale and proportion of the containers and plants should complement their surroundings. Often one large, well-planted container will look better in a small area than an array of smaller containers. Window boxes should match the style of the structure, and the planting should enhance the space from both inside and outside the window. Too much height will block sunlight from the house, but some height in the middle of the box can be a nice touch. Trailing plants look best when they don't touch the ground.

A tall structural plant in a very tall container adds drama to a front yard.

The scale and proportion of your containers should match their surroundings.

Shape

It is important to choose plants with different shapes to provide variety in your container plantings. The careful use of shape can help add drama and emotion or tranquility and peacefulness. Imagine the silhouette of a city skyline and how dull it would look if all the buildings were square blocks of the same size.

Tall, structural plants can be effective on their own, but they also work well as the main feature within a mixed arrangement. Rounded, billowy plants add bulk to a container planting. Short, trailing or mat-forming plants can soften the edges of containers and add depth, as the plants effectively increase the diameter of the container. Short, upright plants are great for filling open spots. Do not forget the shapes of the containers themselves.

Balance

Balance is easy to visualize by thinking of a scale, where what is on one side must balance with what is on the other side. In a design, balanced plantings are pleasing to the eye.

Symmetrical balance: one side is the mirror of the other; often seen in a formal garden.

Asymmetrical balance: the two sides are not the same but have the same visual effect. An example of asymmetrical balance would be a tall, narrow plant flanked by a mid-sized oval plant on one side and a shorter, wider plant on the opposite side.

Radial planting: a central focal point with arms radiating out in all directions. Radial symmetry is achieved when all arms are balanced.

Repetition

When colors or shapes are repeated at intervals throughout the garden, it helps tie the whole design together. Repetition is a design element that is fundamental to many of the great gardens of the world. Whether this is done on a large or small scale, identical repeated plantings can be used to emphasize or exaggerate perspective along a pathway, entrance or succession of steps. A row of identically planted pots can bring a sense of continuity to a space that seems chaotic and unbalanced, but it can also provide appeal to an empty space that begs for a simple focus. Placing a succession of large containers that stand above other in-ground plantings can create a stunning focal point.

Other Design Considerations

Grouping of Containers

Design principles also apply to the grouping and placement of the containers. With careful positioning, a group of varied and different containers can be arranged together for a greater impact. It is a good idea to move the containers slightly away from one another as the plants mature. This allows space between the containers for the plants to fill and enables the sun to reach the leaves.

Containers often look best when placed in a triangular outline. This can be a tall or large container in the middle with smaller pots on each side, or a tall container on one end with successively smaller containers sloping down to the other end. Formal placements often involve an *even* number of containers, such as a pair of square pots marking

the front entrance of a house or two rows of containers forming an allée. Modern, eclectic and contemporary settings are best suited to repeated plantings with an *odd* number of containers as the focal point. A row of hanging plants looks best when all the containers are identical; however, the plantings do not need to be the exactly the same. Cottage gardens, large rustic gardens with wild areas and other informal areas can benefit from a scattering of odd containers.

Adjusting the heights of the pots is another way to create a more luxurious display. Consider raising some of the containers on upturned pots, pot stands or shelves.

Themes

Individual containers and groups of containers can be designed to follow any theme of your choosing—perhaps a Mediterranean theme, a native theme using plants that originate from that area or a tropical theme. A fragrance or aromatherapy garden full of herbs and scented flowers is great for accenting seating areas or for using in window boxes. Each container could include a different scent, which could be easily moved into place to enhance the mood you wish to set, or one large container could have a number or scents within the easy reach of a comfortable chair.

Container gardens lend themselves well to novelty themes, such as a salsa garden, where the plants make up most the ingredients of your recipe, or a theme that integrates the pots into the design, such as different plant hairdos on pots with faces. Container gardening is also well suited to creating cameo gardens, which are small theme gardens in tucked-away places that are somewhat separated from the main garden.

Container Selection

Containers range from fancy pots and urns of all sizes to wooden barrels, planter and window boxes, hanging baskets, washtubs and bathtubs, raised beds, galvanized metal buckets and even a pair of old boots. Anything that is sturdy enough to handle the weight and will not fall over can be used as a container, but keep the following points in mind.

• Bigger is better. A large container is less susceptible to fluctuations in temperature and requires less frequent watering. Larger containers will provide better protection to any bulbs, perennials, trees or shrubs you are going to overwinter. Choose containers that are at least 12" in height and in diameter. Smaller pots can dry out very quickly. They also restrict the root area and reduce the plants' available resources. Deep-rooted plants need deeper pots.

• Ensure that any container you use, regardless of the size, has adequate drainage. Drainage holes are either on the side of the container near the bottom, or on the bottom of the container. Containers can be set on bricks or commercially available pot "feet" to help with drainage. Drainage holes on the bottom of the pot will need to be covered with something to prevent soil loss. Materials such as fine metal or plastic mesh, newspaper, weed barrier, broken clay flowerpot pieces (crocs), coffee filters and cheesecloth are suitable. Many container gardeners will add a 1–2" layer of coarse gravel over the screen to improve drainage, but this is not really necessary anymore because today's plant mixes tend to

A screen will help prevent soil loss through the drainage holes.

drain very well. Using gravel, however, will help keep pots stable and will reduce the amount of planting mix needed in the container.

• Light-colored containers are preferable to dark-colored ones, especially in sunny situations. They will reflect light and will not heat up as much in the sun, especially in spring when overly warm soil can stimulate early plant growth that could be damaged by inclement weather. Preventing container heating also helps prevent roots from cheating or growing to one side of the container. Dark containers are ideal for container garden designs because they provide a visual anchor like no other tone. Just be cautious as to where and when you use them.

• If you plan on moving your containers around, especially large, heavy containers, you may want to have them mounted on wheels. Heavy-duty drip trays, saucers and basic platforms are now available with wheels, allowing you to roll your containers with relative ease. It's recommended that the wheels have a locking mechanism, but it's not always necessary.

• Depending on where your container garden is, e.g., a balcony garden, you may need to use drip trays or saucers underneath your containers. Saucers are useful in dry parts of the country because they help conserve water. Saucers are most often made from clay or synthetic materials. Terra-cotta saucers retain moisture and may damage wood or painted surfaces.

Materials

Containers are constructed from a number of different materials including clay, metal, wood, stone and plastic, fiberglass and other synthetics. Be aware that some materials are more suitable for some parts of our climate than others.

Some materials are more appropriate for certain containers. Window boxes are usually made of wood or plastic.

Unglazed terra-cotta pots (above) and glazed containers (right).

Stone or metal is possible, but weight could be a critical determining factor. Wooden window boxes can be custom built to blend in with the building architecture. Raised beds are built from wood, brick or stone and can also be designed to flow with the building architecture and existing landscape. Hanging baskets are often constructed of wood, plastic or wire, with weight again being a determining factor. There are a number of attractive stands available that provide sturdy support for hanging baskets.

Clay

Clay pots come in two basic forms, glazed and unglazed, in a plethora of shapes and sizes. Clay pots can be heavy, even when they are empty. They are subject to environmental conditions and can be damaged by cold weather. Clay pots require special care, especially in areas that freeze solidly in winter and in areas that experience numerous freeze/thaw cycles.

Terra-cotta containers are porous, which allows plant roots to breathe easily, but it also allows for quick evaporation, so they require frequent monitoring and watering. Terra-cotta holds heat into the night longer than wood, metal or synthetics. Be aware that terra-cotta containers come in different qualities, and you often get what you pay for. Terra-cotta pots from Italy and other Mediterranean countries are usually very good quality. Terra-cotta pots age beautifully over time like no other container material will. Within a few seasons, a combination of salts and organic growth will build on the walls of the pot, resulting in a lovely patina.

Glazed clay containers offer another way to incorporate color into the overall design scheme of your garden. Glazed containers are not porous, so they will need drainage holes on or near the bottom. Glazed pots also benefit from a plastic lining, which helps prevent cracking.

Unglazed clay pots are often referred to as terra-cotta, which simply means "baked earth," referring to the kiln-firing process used in making the pots.

Wood is great for building window boxes.

Wood

Wood offers more insulating value than clay, metal and stone, but it is susceptible to rot, so containers are often lined with plastic or coated with a nontoxic wood preservative. Some woods, such as cedar, are relatively rot resistant. Do not use wood that has been treated with creosote or other toxic substances that can emit compounds that can harm your plants. Wood is adaptable to a variety of climates and can be used across the Midwest. If you have wooden barrels, make sure the hoops and handles are firmly attached. To ensure longevity, particularly at the joints and seams, protect them with wood stain or wood oils, both of which enhance the natural grain and prevent cracking.

Linseed oil is the best oil to use to protect wood that is prone to drying out.

Stone

Stone includes terrazzo, concrete, reconstructed or refurbished stone and natural stone. Stone containers are available in a vast array of shapes, sizes, styles and colors. They tend to be quite heavy and difficult to move. It is best to plant stone containers after they are set in their relatively permanent location, unless they've been placed atop a strong platform or cart with wheels. Stone is often used to accent gardens, and aggregate planters allow stone to be seen on the container surface. Carved stone pots can be very expensive but will add a level of elegance to any formal container garden. A large rock with a trough makes a wonderful place for tiny alpine plants but may need drainage holes drilled through the stone. Stone containers are suitable for all climates and geographic areas.

You can accelerate the aging process on the exterior of your stone containers by simply rubbing a fistful of fresh grass across the surface of the pot. The stain will quickly fade to brown. Brushing a thin layer of yogurt onto a pot's surface will encourage algae and lichen to grow, but a shady and moist location is necessary for the best result.

A stone trough planter (above); a large aggregate container (below).

Metal

Metal containers can be made from tin, copper, bronze, iron, steel or lead and range in shape from simple buckets to fancy, ornate planters and urns. Be aware that metal pots absorb heat like dark-colored containers do. Most metal pots should be lined with plastic or protected from contact with the soil to extend the life of the container. Make sure your metal containers have adequate drainage holes. To protect the drainage holes from rust, apply a coat of anti-rust paint. Plants in plastic containers can be inserted into decorative metal containers rather than using a lining.

Wire is used to make cage-like frames such as hanging baskets, planters and ornate plant stands that can double as planters. These frames are lined with sphagnum moss or some other suitable material before being planted.

To maintain the bright, reflective surfaces of your metal pots, use a soft cloth and window-cleaning spray. Do not use abrasive pads or cleaners. Be careful not to splash water or potting mix onto polished metal; the splashes may leave white calcium deposits, but they can be removed with a soft cloth.

Synthetic

The most commonly used synthetic materials for containers are plastic and fiberglass. These containers come in a vast range of shapes and sizes, from whimsical plastic duck and teddy bear planters to the newer fiberglass containers that resemble good-quality terracotta containers. Synthetic containers are not permeable, so they will need drainage holes. They are lightweight and easy to move with minimal concern for breakage, and most of them are good quality and inexpensive. Lower-quality plastic containers can deteriorate in the sunlight.

Synthetic containers are a good choice for the apartment or condo dweller. They are lightweight and well suited for use on a balcony, and they can be easily moved back and forth seasonally.

Potting-mix stains, dirty handprints and general muck can be easily removed from most synthetic materials by simply using a soft cloth and soapy water. For tougher stains a scouring pad may be necessary, but test a small, hidden area first in case it will damage the surface.

Synthetic containers come in all shapes and sizes.

Container Gardening Environment

Sunlight

Where you place your containers will determine the amount of sunlight they receive. Fortunately, many containers can be easily moved to accommodate the plant's need for more or less sunlight.

Four levels of light may be present in your container garden: full sun, partial shade, light shade and full shade. Available light is affected by the position of the sun depending on the time of day and year, as well as by nearby buildings, trees, fences and other structures.

- Full sun locations, such as along south-facing walls, receive direct sun for at least six hours a day.
- Locations classified as partial shade, such as east- or west-facing walls, receive direct morning or late-afternoon sun and shade for the rest of the day.
- Light shade locations receive shade for most or all of the day, but some sunlight does filter through to ground level. An example of a light-shade location is the ground under a small-leaved tree such as a birch.
- Full shade locations, such as under a dense tree canopy, receive no direct sunlight.

Sun-loving plants may become tall and straggly and flower poorly in too much shade. Shade-loving plants may get scorched leaves, or even wilt and die, if they get too much sun. Many plants tolerate a range of light conditions.

It is important to remember that the intensity of full sun can vary. For example, heat can become trapped and magnified between buildings, baking all but the most heat-tolerant plants. Conversely, a shaded, sheltered space that protects your heat-hating plants in the humid, hot summer may become a frost trap in winter, killing tender plants that should otherwise survive.

Exposure

Your garden is exposed to wind, heat, cold and rain, and some plants are better adapted than others to withstand the potential damage of these forces. Buildings, walls, fences, hills, hedges, trees and even tall perennials often reduce exposure.

Wind and heat are the most likely elements to cause damage to your plants, and cold can affect the survival of perennials, trees and shrubs. The sun can be very intense, and heat can rise quickly on a sunny afternoon, so use plants that tolerate or even thrive in hot weather in the hot spots in your garden. Plants can be dehydrated in windy locations if they aren't able to draw water out of the soil fast enough to replace what is lost through the leaves. Tall, stiff-stemmed plants can be knocked over or broken by strong winds. Some plants that do not require staking in a sheltered location may need to be staked in a more exposed one. Use plants that are recommended for exposed locations, or temper the effect of the wind with hedges or trees. A solid wall creates wind turbulence on the downwind side, while a looser structure, such as a hedge, breaks up the force of the wind and protects a larger area.

A full sun location (above). A dark container in partial shade (below).

All hanging baskets are particularly exposed to wind and heat. Water can evaporate from all sides of a moss basket, and in hot or windy locations, moisture can be depleted very quickly. Watch for wilting and water regularly. Wire baskets will hold up better in adverse conditions if you soak the moss or other

Hanging baskets are often very exposed to the environment.

liner in a commercially available wetting agent, which can be organic, and add some of the wetting agent to the water when first watering. Hanging baskets are a great place to add water-holding polymers to the planting mix.

One drop of a mild liquid dish detergent in one quart of water is a useful and cost-efficient wetting agent. The soap breaks down the surface tension of the water, which allows it to penetrate the material rather than just roll over the outer edge. This is helpful when you're unable to find wetting agents at your garden center.

Too much rain can damage some plants, as can overwatering. Established plants (or their flowers) can be destroyed by heavy rain. Most plants will recover, but some are slow to do so. Grow-covers are used to build temporary greenhouses, usually with a couple of wire hoops placed over the container and a light, white fabric covering placed over the wires, which allows sun, air and moisture in and keeps bugs, birds and wet weather out. For exposed sites, choose plants or varieties that are quick to recover from rain damage. Many of the small-flowered petunia varieties and new petunia cultivars recover well from the effects of heavy rain.

Frost Dates and Hardiness Zones

You will need to be aware of frost dates and hardiness zones. When planting annuals, consider their ability to tolerate an unexpected frost. Last-frost and first-frost dates vary greatly from year to year and region to region. They can also vary considerably within each region. Consult your local garden center for more specific information.

Annuals are grouped into three categories based on how tolerant they are of cold weather: hardy, half-hardy or tender.

- Hardy annuals tolerate low temperatures and even frost. They can be placed in your containers early in the year and may continue to flower long into fall or even winter. Many hardy annuals can be seeded directly into containers before the last spring frost date.
- Half-hardy annuals can tolerate a light frost. These annuals can be planted into your containers around the last-frost date and will generally benefit from being started early from seed indoors, such as those transplants available from garden centers.

- Tender annuals have no frost tolerance at all and might suffer if the temperature drops to even a few degrees above freezing. These plants are often started early indoors and should not be planted into your containers until the last-frost date has passed and the potting mix has had a chance to warm. These annuals often have the advantage of tolerating hot summer temperatures.

Perennials, bulbs, trees and shrubs have a minimum temperature for survival and will have a hardiness zone designation. These plants will die if the

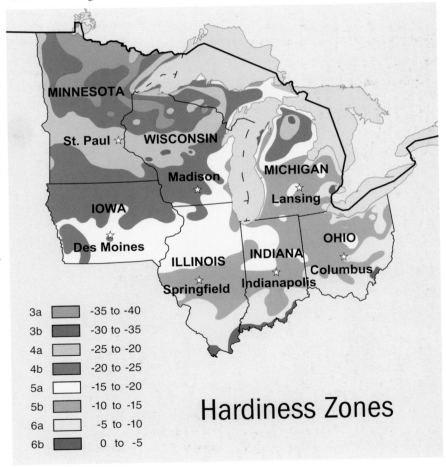

Zone	Temperature
3a	-35 to -40
3b	-30 to -35
4a	-25 to -20
4b	-20 to -25
5a	-15 to -20
5b	-10 to -15
6a	-5 to -10
6b	0 to -5

Hardiness Zones

Trees and stairwells can create a microclimate for your containers.

on the average lowest winter temperatures. Mild or harsh winters, heavy or light snow cover, fall care and the overall health of the plants that you grow all influence their ability to live through winter.

Also, local topography in the garden creates microclimates—small areas that may be more or less favorable for growing different plants. Microclimates may be created, for example, in the shelter of a nearby building or a stand of evergreen trees, in a low, still hollow or the top of a barren, windswept hill or near a large body of water. Because of the exposure of a container, experts recommend plants that are hardy to one zone beyond yours—try to overwinter Zone 4 plants if you live in Zone 5, for instance. Container gardening with plants that are borderline hardy is a challenging and fun part of gardening. Always continue to experiment and explore.

plants experience a prolonged spell of colder weather. The USDA created the hardiness zone map based on minimum average winter temperatures and plant survival data. Many plants also have a maximum temperature threshold, above which the plants may die. Our area has a wide range of hardiness zones, and you will need to know your zone. If you're not sure, ask an employee at your local nursery or a savvy gardener friend.

Don't feel intimidated or limited by the information you find on hardiness zones. The divisions are based mostly

Nasturtiums and dahlias are tender plants that appreciate protection from frost.

Perennials and shrubs for sale.

Container Principles

Choosing Healthy Plants

Many gardeners consider the trip to the local garden center an important rite of spring. Others consider starting their own plants from seed one of the most rewarding aspects of gardening. Both methods have benefits, and many gardeners use a combination of the two.

Purchasing plants is usually easier than starting from seed and provides you with plants that are well grown and often already in bloom. Starting seeds can be fun but requires space, facilities and time. Some seeds require specific conditions difficult to achieve in a house, or they have erratic germination rates. Other seeds are easy and inexpensive to start. Starting from seed offers you a greater selection because seed catalogues have many more varieties available than what are offered at most garden centers.

Most plants get established and grow quickly once they are planted in your containers. Plants are sold in individual pots and in divided cell-packs. Each type has its advantages and disadvantages.
• Plants in individual pots are usually well established, having been nurtured along in the nursery, and have plenty of space for root growth. The cost of labor, pots and soil can be expensive if you are purchasing a large number of plants.

The plant on the right is much healthier than the plant on the left (above). A root-bound rootball (below).

• Annuals, biennials and perennials grown in cell-packs are often inexpensive and hold several plants. These plants suffer minimal root damage when transplanted, but because each cell is quite small, plants may become root-bound quickly and should be planted soon after you've purchased them. Although smaller plants are more economical in the long run, it will take them longer to fill the container.

It is usually best to purchase plants that haven't yet flowered, but this isn't always a possibility, as many plants are strategically grown to be flowering as early as possible for the garden centers. Plants that haven't yet flowered are younger and less likely to be root-bound. Plants covered with an abundance of flowers or flower buds have already passed through a significant portion of their rooting stage, and while they will add instant color when planted, they will not perform at their best in the heat of summer, and their longevity can be compromised. Now this is not to say that you shouldn't consider blooming plants for your containers, but if you choose to buy annuals or perennials already in bloom, pinch off the blooms and buds just prior to planting. This encourages new root growth and a bigger show of flowers throughout the season.

Check for roots emerging from the holes at the bottom of the cells, or gently remove the plant from the container to look at the roots. An overabundance of roots means that the plant is too mature for the container, especially if the roots wrapped around the inside of the container resemble a thick web. Such plants are slow to establish once they are transplanted. Healthy roots will appear almost white. Avoid potted plants with very dark, spongy roots that pull away with little effort.

Plants should be compact and have good color. Healthy leaves look firm and vibrant. Check carefully for diseases and insects.

Once you get your plants home, water them if they are dry. Plants growing in small containers may require watering more than once a day. Keep them in a lightly shaded location until you plant them. Remove any damaged growth.

Get your plants from a reputable source, especially trees, shrubs and perennials. Locally sourced plants will survive in your area better than plants imported from another state or country. Garden centers, mail-order catalogues, friends, family and neighbors are other sources for plants. A number of garden societies promote the exchange of plants and seeds, and many public gardens sell seeds of rare plants. Gardening clubs are also a great source for rare and unusual plants.

Staff at nurseries and garden centers should be able to answer questions and make recommendations. It will be helpful to them if you bring an overhead sketch of the area where you intend to have your container garden and mark potential locations of the containers. Be sure to mark shaded areas, windy areas, garden and structure orientation (north, south, etc.) and so forth on the sketch so that they can help you choose appropriate plants. You will also find it convenient to take this book to the nursery. You'll have information about the plants and photos of them at your fingertips as you browse.

Preparing Containers for Planting

Container Cleaning

Starting with a clean container is important for minimizing soil-borne plant diseases and for removing deposits from fertilizers and plant root compounds released by the plant into the surrounding soil. Even new containers

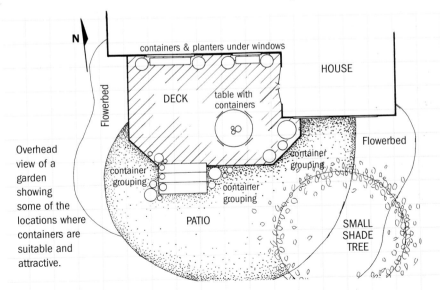

Overhead view of a garden showing some of the locations where containers are suitable and attractive.

N

containers & planters under windows

HOUSE

Flowerbed

DECK

table with containers

Flowerbed

container grouping

container grouping

container grouping

PATIO

SMALL SHADE TREE

should be cleaned to remove any dust from transport and handling. Most containers are easily cleaned with mild soap and water with a good rinsing.

Terra-cotta pots require a different cleaning process. Soak the containers overnight or longer in a solution of nine parts water to one part bleach. Soaking the containers for a longer period of time makes the pots easier to clean. Use a plastic bucket appropriate for the size of container you are cleaning. Use a wire or stiff-bristle plastic brush to scrub the inside of the container. Deposits can be scraped off with a knife or other appropriate scraping tool. Soak the scrubbed container in clean water for 15 minutes to remove the bleach and then give it a quick spray rinse. If you are cleaning glazed containers, make sure the bleach will not damage the glaze.

Container Drainage

If your container does not have adequate drainage, you run the risk of drowning your plants. Some form of opening in the bottom of containers is essential for good drainage. Extra holes may need to be made in some containers that do not drain as quickly as needed.

Containers that have no drainage, or very minimal drainage, can be used to grow plants that do well in boggy conditions, such as those found along stream banks, ponds and other water features.

Decorative containers can be used just as they would indoors, where a planted pot is set into a decorative pot.

Ensure that water is never allowed to collect or pool between the two pots; otherwise, the rootball will become waterlogged and begin to rot. This arrangement is recommended only for smaller containers.

Choosing an Appropriate Planting Mix

Many plants need soil that allows excess water to drain away but still retains enough water and nutrients for the plants to use. Commercially available container planting mixes allow good drainage, are lighter in weight than garden soils, have nutrient-holding capacity and do not have soil-borne diseases or weed seeds. Avoid using garden soil because it drains poorly and tends to dry into a solid mass. A small amount of good garden soil can be mixed into the planting mix, which adds minerals and microorganisms and improves the nutrient holding capacity, but it may also be introducing soil-borne diseases. There are a variety of mixes available depending on what properties your soil needs to have for the plants you want to grow.

Many commercial planting mixes now contain compost in varying percentages. High-quality compost should be an integral part of every container planting mix. Water-holding polymers are already mixed into some commercial potting mixes.

Regular commercial planting mixes are mainly peat moss or coir fiber and can contain tree bark, vermiculite, perlite, dolomite lime, sterilized loam or clay, superphosphate for quick rooting and often some form of slow-release fertilizer. Coir fiber is made from the husks of coconuts. It is more environmentally friendly than peat moss but can be

A selection of planting mixes.

Reducing the Weight of Your Containers

If weight is an issue, consider these steps:

- Do not use gravel in the bottom of the containers and do not use planting mixes that contain soil or sand.
- If you will be planting only annuals in larger containers, some of the planting mix in the bottom half can be replaced with Styrofoam packing peanuts, broken pieces Styrofoam packing from goods such as electronic products, well-crushed pieces of newspaper or shredded leaves, or you can use flipped over plastic pots set in place before the planting mix is added.

Perennials and shrubs may need all the container space filled with soil for roots to grow in. Be sure not to lighten the pot so dramatically that it becomes unstable with the mass of the plant.

harder to handle. Commercially available organic plant mixes are available in different formulations depending on what the manufacturer chooses to use in the product. They are mainly peat moss or coir fiber and may contain high-quality compost, composted leaf mold, bone meal, blood meal, humus, earthworm castings, bird or bat guano, glacial rock dust, dolomite lime, pulverized oyster shells, alfalfa meal, rock phosphate, greensand, kelp meal and beneficial mycorrhizal fungi.

If you have a lot of containers, there are large bags and bales of commercial planting mix available. You can also make your own from bulk ingredients to reduce costs. For the mix, we suggest using 40% sphagnum peat moss or coir, 40% high-quality compost, 10% garden loam and 10% washed and screened coarse, angular sand. You can add high-phosphorous guano or bone meal for a root booster, or you can mix in a commercially formulated organic fertilizer. For those plants that require an alkaline soil, dolomite lime or oyster shells can be mixed in to raise the pH. Add these fertilizer products as instructed on the product label for the volume of soil your containers will use. A soil test is a useful tool for determining what additions and adjustments your planting mix might need.

Planting Your Containers

Generally, you can transplant into containers at the same time you would in a regular garden. There is a proper order to plant into containers. For plants, it is trees first, then shrubs, bulbs, perennials and finally annuals. For size, the largest plants go in first and work down in size to the smallest plants.

- Fill your cleaned container with moistened planting mix until it is approximately 75% filled. Place the plants into their respective positions to check your arrangement before removing them from the nursery pots.
- After removing the plants from their pots, gently tease the outside of the rootballs apart, or if the plant is rootbound, score the outer roots with a sharp knife to encourage the roots to spread out rather than continue to coil into a mass.
- Install trellises, stakes or other supports that are needed.

A selection of plants for a new container (top). Place mesh screen over drainage holes (bottom).

Terra-cotta pots should be soaked before planting. Given its porosity, the clay will draw the moisture out of the soil and away from your new plants.

Fill the container with an appropriate amount of planting mix (above). Place potted plants in the container to check placement (center).

Remove plants from their pots and deal with any excess roots (below).

- Place the larger, central focal plants into the container first, followed by the smaller ones.
- Don't plant too deeply or too shallowly. Use the depth at which the plants are already growing as a guide for how deeply they should be planted. You don't want to have exposed roots above soil level, but you don't want to bury the crowns, which can lead to rot. If you're adding seeds to the mix, then do so at this stage. Plant them at the depth recommended on the package.
- Add more potting mix, as necessary, to surround the rootballs of the plants.
- Add the smallest and outer-edge plants last and top up the potting mix, allowing at least two inches from the top edge of the pot for watering and perhaps a layer of decorative mulch.
- Ensure the planting mix is without gaps or air pockets in between or under the plants. This can be done by gently tapping the bottom of the pot on the ground or by slipping your hand into the potting mix to move the soil into gaps and pockets.
- Watering will also encourage the potting mix to settle without having to firm it down with your hands. Water until the container is thoroughly soaked.
- Add more planting mix if it settles too much after the first soaking.

How many plants to include in a container is a matter of preference, but overplanted containers look better than having a small number of plants. This does not apply to specimen plants in their own containers. The spacing between plants in containers can be reduced from what is noted on the plant tag. However, too many plants in one container will be forced to compete with each other for space, water, nutrients and light, so you will still need some soil

Tease out some of the roots on the bottom of the root ball (top & left).

Make sure each plant has enough room (bottom left).

Water the freshly planted container immediately (below).

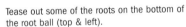

between each plant to provide room for their roots to spread. Be aware that with more plants in a container, you will have to apply more water and fertilizer.

Water plants regularly when they are first planted. Containers can dry out quickly, and newly planted plants need to become established before they can tolerate adverse conditions.

We encourage you to make detailed notes and planting diagrams for each container, including when the container was planted and the common and scientific name of each plant for future reference. This is especially helpful when you want to replicate or avoid what you planted from one year to the next, based on your successes and failures.

Planting Trees and Specimen Plants

Ensure that the container is of sufficient size to allow for root growth and to include enough planting mix to insulate the roots and crown from extreme climate conditions. Planting mixes for trees benefit from having garden loam as part of the mix. This makes the container more stable and gives the tree roots something a little more solid to root into.

Most plants, especially trees, shrubs and perennials, should be planted in spring to early summer to allow them enough time to become established before facing a cold winter. This is, of course, if you want to overwinter hardy plants in their containers. Some gardeners prefer to keep the hardier plants in the containers only for the growing season, with plans to plant them in the ground later on. Others simply treat these plants as annuals.

Container Garden Maintenance

Your container garden will need regular maintenance just like regular gardens, but on a much-reduced scale. The most important tasks are watering and feeding. Weeding, grooming, relieving soil compaction and repotting are other tasks that require some attention. You will need a minimal selection of quality tools including a hand trowel, a hand cultivator, a watering can with a diffuser and by-pass hand pruners.

Watering

Watering is the most important maintenance task you will perform. Watering cans or buckets are good if you have only a small number of containers. Rainbarrels are great places to fill watering cans and buckets. Watering cans come with a diffuser that turns the

water flow into a gentle rain shower, which helps minimize soil compaction and keeps tender plant shoots from being broken. A hose with a watering wand is effective for a larger number of containers. Both of these methods are

Water until it drains freely out the drainage holes.

Organic amendments (left to right): moisture-holding granules, earthworm castings, glacial dust, mycorrhizae, bat guano, compost, bone meal and coir fibre.

time consuming but allow you to visit and inspect your containers regularly. You can use commercially available water-holding polymers, which are mixed into the planting mix and act as a moisture reservoir, to reduce your watering time and cost.

Small containers, hanging baskets and terra-cotta pots may need to be watered twice daily during hot, sunny and/or windy weather. Water until the entire planting mix is thoroughly soaked and water runs out of the drainage holes.

To check if the container needs water, first feel the surface. If it is dry, poke your finger a couple of inches into the planting mix. If it still feels dry, it is time to water. You can also lift the container off the ground a little, and if it feels light, it needs to be watered.

If the soil in your container dries out, you will have to water several times to make sure water is absorbed throughout the planting medium. A good method is to place the whole container in a bucket of water until the surface of the planting mix feels moist.

To save time, money and water, or if you plan to be away from your garden for an extended period, consider installing a drip irrigation system. These systems apply water in a slow, steady trickle, which takes longer than watering with a can or hose but still thoroughly soaks the containers. Drip irrigation reduces the amount of water lost to evaporation. Systems can be fully automated with timers and moisture sensors. Consult with your local garden center or irrigation professionals for more information.

You can lower your watering requirements by adding a thin layer of mulch to each container. You can also group containers together to aid in the reduction of evaporation from each container. Placing containers in sheltered locations can also reduce evaporation.

Feeding

Plants in containers have limited access to nutrients. Your plants will need a boost during the growing season, and you will have to apply some form of fertilizer. Plants that are heavy feeders will definitely need additional supplements.

Commercially available fertilizer comes in various forms including liquids, water-soluble powders, slow-release granules or pellets and bulk materials such as compost. Follow the package directions carefully because using too much fertilizer can kill your plants by burning their roots. If you use a good-quality planting mix that has compost and an organic or slow-release fertilizer mixed in, you may not need to add extra fertilizer.

Many plants will flower most profusely if they have access to enough nutrients. Some gardeners fertilize hanging baskets and container gardens every time they water, using a very diluted fertilizer so as not to burn the roots. Too much fertilizer stimulates excessive plant growth and can result in lanky stems and weak or overly lush plant growth that is susceptible to pest and disease problems. Some plants, such as nasturtiums, grow better without fertilizer and may produce few or no flowers when fertilized excessively.

Healthy soil allows plants to grow better over the course of summer. Organic fertilizers enhance the microorganism population in the planting mix, which in turn makes more nutrients available to the plants. Organic fertilizers don't work as quickly as many inorganic fertilizers, but they often don't leach out as quickly. They can be watered into planting mix or used as a foliar spray as often as weekly.

Organic fertilizers can be simple or complex formulations. They may include alfalfa pellets, well-composted animal manure, crab meal, coconut meal, corn gluten, kelp meal, sunflower meal, rock phosphate, humus, leaf mold, bone meal, blood meal, earthworm castings, bird or bat guano, dolomite lime,

Pinching off a spent bloom.

pulverized oyster shells, glacial rock dust, greensand and beneficial mycorrhizal fungi. Be aware that bonemeal, fish emulsion and other odorous organic fertilizers may attract unwanted garden visitors that can cause some major destruction.

Containerized trees and shrubs benefit from the annual removing of some of the planting mix from the container and topping up the container with fresh, good-quality compost.

Weeding

Weeding your containers is easiest when the weeds are small. Well-planted containers often exclude enough sunlight to suppress weed growth. Don't forget about the weeds that pop up around your containers.

Grooming

Good grooming helps keep your container plants healthy and neat, makes them flower more profusely and helps prevent many pest and disease problems. Grooming may include pinching, trimming, staking, deadheading, training

Don't be afraid to trim any plant that is exceeding its boundaries (above).

vines and climbing plants and pruning trees and shrubs.

Pinching refers to removing by hand or with scissors any straggly growth and the tips of leggy plants. Plants in cell-packs may develop tall and straggly growth in an attempt to get light. Pinch back long stems when transplanting to encourage bushier growth. Remove any yellow or dying leaves. Pinch back excess growth from more robust plants if they are overwhelming their less vigorous container mates. Keep trailing stems from touching the ground.

If annuals appear tired and withered by mid-summer, try trimming them back to encourage a second bloom. Mounding or low-growing annuals, such as petunias, respond well to trim-ming. Use garden shears and trim back a quarter to half of the plant growth. New growth will sprout along with a second flush of flowers. Give the plants a light fertilizing as well at this time.

Some plants have very tall growth and cannot be pinched or trimmed. Instead, remove the main shoot after it blooms, and side shoots may develop.

Tall plants may require staking. Tie plants loosely to tall, thin stakes with soft ties that won't cut into the plant. Narrow ties are less visible. Stake bushy plants with twiggy branches. Insert the twigs into the planting mix near the plant when it is small, and as the plant grows, it will hide the twigs. A careful selection of twiggy branches can add another attractive dimension to your containers.

Vines in containers can be used as trailers or trained to climb up trellises, netting or other structures. The struc-ture can be inserted into the container, or the container can be placed near the structure. Vines with tendrils climb best on structures that are small enough in diameter for the their tendrils to easily wrap around, such as a cage-like trellis or netting. Other climbers will need to be woven through or tied to their struc-tures. Do not be afraid to clip off any rampant or out-of-bounds growth.

Learn proper pruning techniques before trimming trees and shrubs.

Many annuals and perennials benefit from deadheading (removing faded flowers), which often helps prolong their bloom time. Deadheading keeps the plants and your containers looking their best and prevents containers from becoming a seed bank. Decaying flowers can harbor pests and diseases, so it is a good habit to pick off spent flowers when you are checking your containers. Some plants, such as impatiens and wax begonias, are self-cleaning or self-grooming, meaning that they drop their faded blossoms on their own. Leaving the seedheads on other plants, such as ornamental grasses, can provide winter interest.

Trees and shrubs will need to be pruned to keep them healthy and in proportion to the container. Each tree or shrub will have its own pruning requirements, such as the best time to prune and how much of the plant can be safely removed. It is important to learn where, when and how to make proper pruning cuts. There are books available that describe proper pruning techniques, and classes on pruning are available from horticultural college and university extension programs and public gardens.

Relieving Soil Compaction

Planting mixes in containers can experience soil compaction from the effects of constant watering. A hardened crust can form on the surface that does

Trees, shrubs and perennials will eventually outgrow their containers.

not allow water and air to penetrate into the planting mix, which can be easily broken up with a good hand cultivator. Replace the top layer of planting mix annually in spring.

Repotting Plants

Trees, shrubs and perennials can stay in containers for a number of years with proper care and maintenance. At some point, the plants will become rootbound and will need repotting. Perennials should be divided at this time, and trees and shrubs will need their roots pruned.

Perennials need dividing when flowering is diminished, when the plant loses vigor, when the center of the plant has died out or when the plant encroaches on the other plants in the container. Replant perennial divisions as soon as possible. Extra divisions can be spread around into other containers, shared with friends or composted. Trees and shrubs that need repotting will also appear less vigorous and have reduced flowering.

The rule of thumb for choosing new containers is to use the next larger size. Perennials will be divided, so they may not need a larger container. Trees and shrubs will require containers only a couple of inches wider and deeper than their current containers, and they will need some root pruning. Using too large a container can cause overwatering problems.

Tree and shrub containers can be heavy, and you may need help to tip over the container. You may want to wrap the branches in a blanket to prevent damage to the plant before you tip the container. Gently remove the plant and shake off some of the old planting mix. Tease out the larger roots that are encircling the container or growing in toward the center of the root mass and cut them off where they would have just touched the edges of the previous container. When tree roots are pruned or damaged, the plant responds by reducing its top growth. Allow the plants to do this naturally; wait and then prune off the dead branches when they become visible rather than pruning immediately. Replant the tree or shrub into its new home with fresh planting mix, ensuring it is firmly settled with no air pockets.

The top growth (leaves, twigs and branches) of trees and shrubs produces hormones that stimulate root growth, and the roots produce hormones that stimulate top growth.

Protecting Containers and Plants

Insulating Containers

Some plants prefer a cool, moist root environment during the heat of summer, and some plants need extra protection from the effects of winter. Containers can be insulated in similar fashion for both situations. Rot-resistant wood such as cedar makes an attractive container that offers protection from excessive heating and cooling. Other containers may need help keeping the roots cool. One container placed into another with a minimum of one inch of space between the containers for insulating material such as moistened vermiculite, sawdust or Styrofoam packing peanuts is effective. The inside of a container may be lined with stiff foam insulation for straight-sided containers or lined with a couple of layers of carpet underlay for curved-sided containers.

You can also use a few overlapping layers of bubble wrap in warmer parts of the Midwest.

Protecting Containers from Frost Damage

Clay containers are subject to frost damage. Any water that has been absorbed by the container will expand as it freezes, causing cracks and chips. Avoid any containers with narrow openings. When moist soil in the container is subjected to freezing temperatures it will expand, which can crack even the most sturdy clay or stone container. An opening that is equal to or larger than the rest of the container will allow freezing soil to expand upward rather than out.

Protecting Tender Plants

Protecting plants from frost is relatively simple. Cover them overnight with sheets, towels, burlap, row covers or even cardboard boxes. Don't use plastic

because it doesn't retain heat and therefore won't provide your plants with any insulation. You can also move your containers to a frost-free area (garage, garden shed or greenhouse).

Tender plants, including tropicals, may have to be moved indoors in winter. Tender, evergreen plants can be lifted or dug from their respective containers, repotted and brought into the shelter of a greenhouse or the sunniest, warmest location in your house before the first frosts occur in fall. Most tender plants can be treated as houseplants, whether they return outdoors the following season or not. If you're without space to overwinter large, tender plants indoors, cuttings can be taken in late summer and grown as smaller plants for the following spring.

Some gardeners will grow their tender plants in partial shade outdoors so that the plants will be used to the lower light levels when brought inside for the winter season. This applies to plants that you wish to be ornamental inside your home as well as outside.

Terra-cotta pots are subject to frost and cold damage.

This might not be the best storage for terra-cotta containers (left). Make sure the container is big enough to protect the plant's roots (right).

Preparing for Winter

Storing Containers

Containers that will be emptied at the end of the growing season can be cleaned and moved to a suitable storage spot. This will help prolong the life of the containers. Containers that can't be moved and have no plants can be emptied of planting mix and cleaned. Ensure all containers are in good condition, and if needed, repairs can be done during the winter months. In areas that experience freezing temperatures, clay containers, especially decorative glazed

containers, should be emptied of soil and stored indoors.

Overwintering Hardy Trees, Shrubs and Perennials

Hardy trees, shrubs and perennials that you intend to overwinter will survive better if the plants are allowed to harden as winter approaches. This means reducing the amount of water and fertilizer the plants receive through late summer and fall, which signals the plants to prepare themselves for the coming cold weather.

When the outside temperature drops below 32° F, planting mix can freeze solid. Plants continue to use water throughout winter, and even hardy plants can be killed, as frozen planting mix does not allow the plants to take up moisture. Containers that have a large enough volume of planting mix will increase the chances of the plants surviving winter. Water dry containers as soon as the planting mix thaws.

Overwintering Tender Rhizomes, Bulbs, Corms and Tubers

Perennials that grow from tender rhizomes, bulbs, corms or tubers can be dug up in fall after the top growth dies back, stored over winter and replanted in spring. If there is a chance that the container may freeze, dig up the tubers, bulbs, rhizomes, or corms before that can happen. Shake the loose dirt from the roots and let them dry in a cool, dark place. Once dry, the rest of the soil should brush away. You can dust these modified underground stems with an antifungal powder such as garden sulfur (found at garden centers) before storing them in moist peat moss or coarse sawdust. Keep them in a cool, dark, dry place that doesn't freeze. Check on them once a month, and lightly spray the storage medium with water if they appear very dry. If they start to sprout, pot them and keep them in moist soil in a bright window. They should be potted by late winter or early spring so that they will be ready for the outdoors. Some gardeners will leave the tubers in the containers and store the whole containers inside over winter.

Pests and Diseases

Your container garden may experience attacks from pests and diseases. This need not be a traumatic event, as there are numerous ways of dealing with any problems that arise. You should not have to worry about soil-borne pests and diseases; they are almost non-existent in container gardens, especially when using soil-less planting mixes.

Annuals are planted each spring, and different species are often grown each year, so it can be difficult for pests and diseases to find their preferred host plants and establish a population. However, if you grow a lot of one particular species, any problems that do set in over summer may attack all the plants.

Perennials, trees and shrubs are both an asset and a liability when it comes to

pests and diseases. Containers often contain a mixture of different plant species. Because many insects and diseases attack only one species of plant, mixed containers make it difficult for pests and diseases to settle in. But the plants are in the same container for a number of years, and any problems that do develop can become permanent. Yet, if allowed, beneficial insects, birds and other pest-devouring organisms can also develop permanent populations.

Integrated Pest Management (IPM) is a moderate approach for dealing with pests and diseases. The goal of IPM is to reduce pest problems to levels of damage acceptable to you. Attempting to totally eradicate pests is a futile endeavor. Consider whether a pest's

Aphids.

Adult ladybird beetle.

damage is localized or covers the entire plant. Will the damage kill the plant, or is it only affecting the outward appearance? Can the pest be controlled without chemicals?

IPM includes learning about your plants and the conditions they need for healthy growth. Some plant problems arise from poor maintenance practices. For example, overwatering saps plants of energy and can cause yellowing of the plant from the bottom up.

It is also useful for you to learn what pests might affect your plants, where and when to look for those pests and how to control them. Keep records of pest damage because your observations can reveal patterns useful in spotting recurring problems and in planning your maintenance regime.

Prevention and Control

The first line of defense for your plants is to prevent pests and diseases from attacking in the first place. The best way to accomplish this is to provide the conditions necessary for healthy plant growth. Healthy plants are able to fend well for themselves and can sustain some damage. Plants that are stressed or weakened are more prone to attack. Keep your soil healthy by using plenty of good-quality compost. Spray your

Powdery mildew.

Ladybird beetle larva.

plant's foliage with high-quality, fungally-dominated compost tea or fish emulsion. This acts as a foliar feed and also prevents against fungal diseases.

Other cultural practices can help prevent pest attacks:

• Provide enough space for your plants so that they have good air circulation and are not stressed from competing for available resources.

• Remove plants that have been decimated by pests and dispose of diseased foliage and branches.

• Keep your gardening tools clean and tidy up fallen leaves and dead plant matter in and around your permanently planted containers at the end of every growing season.

Physical controls are generally used to combat insect and mammal problems. An example of such a control is picking insects off plants by hand, which is easy if you catch the problem when it is just beginning. Large, slow insects are particularly easy to pick off. You can squish or rub off colonies of insects with your fingers. Other physical controls include traps, barriers, scarecrows and natural repellants that make a plant taste or smell bad to pests. Garden centers offer a wide array of such devices. Physical control of diseases usually involves removing the infected plant or parts of the plant in order to keep the problem from spreading.

Biological controls make use of populations of natural predators. Birds, spiders and many insects help keep pest populations at a manageable level. Encourage these creatures to take up permanent residence in or near your garden, even though it may be difficult

Green lacewings are beneficial predators.

on balcony and rooftop gardens. Bird-baths and feeders encourage birds to visit your container garden and feed on a wide variety of insect pests. Many beneficial insects are already living in or near your garden, and you can encourage them to stay and multiply by planting appropriate food sources. Many beneficial insects eat nectar from flowers.

Chemical controls should be used only as a last resort. Pesticide products can be either organic or synthetic. If you have tried the other suggested methods and still wish to take further action, try to use organic types, which are available at most garden centers.

Chemical or organic pesticides may also kill the beneficial insects you have been trying to attract. Many people think that because a pesticide is organic, they can use however much they want. An organic spray kills because it contains a lethal toxin. NEVER overuse any pesticide. When using pesticides, follow the manufacturer's instructions carefully and apply in the recommended amounts only to the pests listed on the label. A large amount of pesticide is not any more effective in controlling pests than the recommended amount.

PROVEN WINNERS

PROVEN WINNERS

About This Guide

This book showcases 100 plants suitable for container gardening in the Midwest. The plants are organized alphabetically by their most familiar common names. Scientific or botanical names appear in italics after the primary reference, and additional common names, if they exist, are listed with the features of each entry. This system enables gardeners who are familiar with only the common name of a plant to find that plant easily in the book. However, you are strongly encouraged to learn the botanical name. Common names are sometimes shared by several different plants, and they can change from region to region. Only the botanical name defines the specific plant everywhere on the planet.

The illustrated **Plants at a Glance** section at the beginning of the book allows you to quickly familiarize yourself with the different plants, and it will help you find a plant if you're unsure of its name.

Clearly indicated within each entry are the plant's outstanding features, height and spread ranges, hardiness zone(s) and grow rating. At the back of the book, a **Quick Reference Chart** summarizes different features and requirements of the plants; you will find this chart handy when planning what is best for your container gardening designs.

Each entry gives clear instructions for growing the plant in a container garden and recommends many of our favorite selections. Note: if height and spread ranges or hardiness zones are not given for each recommended plant, assume these values are the same as the ranges given with the features of the entry. If unsure, check with your local garden center experts when making your selections.

PROVEN WINNERS (OPPOSITE PAGE)

Plant Directory

African Daisy
Osteospermum

O. SOPRANO LIGHT PURPLE from the Proven Winners Selection SOPRANO SERIES

You may find African daisy listed as either Dimorphotheca *or* Osteospermum. Dimorphotheca *is a closely related genus that formerly included all the plants now listed as* Osteospermum.

Features: white, peach, orange, yellow, pink, lavender or purple flowers, often with darker centers **Height:** 12–20" **Spread:** 10–20" **Hardiness:** perennial or subshrub grown as an annual **Grow rating:** medium

Electric blue-purple centers set these daisy-like flowers apart. Originally intolerant of mid-summer heat, newer series such as Symphony continue their robust spring bloom cycle through summer. Look for them in garden centers again in late summer when you need something that blooms well into cooler weather.

Growing
African daisy grows best in **full sun**. The potting mix should be **light, moist** and **well drained**. Fertilize every two weeks with half-strength fertilizer. Deadhead to encourage new growth and more flowers. Young plants can be pinched to encourage bushiness.

Tips
African daisy's flowers mix well with other annuals such as petunia and verbena, or plant it with other daisy-like flowers for a daisy-themed container.

Recommended
O. ecklonis can grow upright to almost prostrate. The species is almost never grown in favor of its cultivars. **'Passion Mix'** includes heat-tolerant plants with pink, rose, purple or white flowers with deep blue centers. It was an All-America Selections winner in 1999. **Starwhirls Series** has unique, spoon-shaped petals.

O. SOPRANO SERIES are robust, upright but compact plants that have regular or spoon-shaped petals in white and shades of purple.

O. **Symphony Series** are mound-forming, heat-tolerant plants. **'Lemon'** bears yellow flowers. **'Orange'** bears tangerine orange flowers. **'Peach'** bears peachy pink flowers. **'Vanilla'** bears white flowers.

Alternanthera
Alternanthera

The unique colors and foliage of these non-flowering plants make ordinary combinations special. Related to amaranths, alternantheras range in color from the brightest reds to deep purples.

Growing

Alternanthera develops the best leaf color when grown in **full sun** but tolerates partial shade. Most potting mixes will work, as long as they are **moist** and **well drained**. Fertilize monthly with half-strength fertilizer. Pinch the plant tips or shear lightly to encourage bushy growth. Bring plants indoors before the first frost and place in a sunny window if you intend to overwinter them.

Tips

Alternanthera's foliage adds bright splashes of color in mixed container plantings and provides great contrast when paired with plants that are lighter in color. Look for the cultivar 'Red Threads' to act as a filler or spiller in a pot or hanging basket.

Recommended

A. dentata is an upright, spreading plant with dark green foliage often tinted red or purple. It grows about 18–20" tall. **'Purple Knight'** has very dark burgundy-purple foliage. **'Rubignosa'** (indoor clover) has burgundy-red leaves that are green underneath.

A. ficoidea (Joseph's coat, parrot leaf) is a bushy, rounded plant that grows 6–12" tall. It has brightly colored, variegated leaves and insignificant flowers. Cultivars may have green or bronze leaves marked with red, pink, purple, orange or yellow. **'Red Threads'** has very narrow, grass-like, deep burgundy foliage.

A. ficoidea

Features: green or bronze leaves marked with red, pink, yellow, purple or orange **Height:** 6–20" **Spread:** 12–18" or more **Hardiness:** tender perennial grown as an annual **Grow rating:** easy

Arborvitae
Thuja

T. plicata SPRING GROVE

Arborvitae can usually only be grown in containers for three to five years, after which it will need to be planted in the ground, or it is likely to die.

Also called: cedar **Features:** evergreen shrub or small tree **Height:** 18"–10' **Spread:** 18"–4' **Hardiness:** zones 3–8 **Grow rating:** easy

This soft-needled evergreen is available in all sizes for container growing. Many can be shaped to fit an architectural setting. The larger the container the better, because this woody plant consumes a lot of water.

Growing

Arborvitae grows well in **full sun, partial shade** or **light shade** in a sheltered location. The potting mix should be **moist** and **well drained**. Keep plants well watered. Fertilize with a weak fertilizer no more than monthly in spring and early summer. Overwinter outdoors in a location out of strong winds and bright sun. Both can dry out the foliage and kill the plant.

Tips

Arborvitae is popular for use as a screening plant on decks and patios. Although it can be combined with flowering perennials and annuals, it is often most effective as a specimen in its own pot. Several can be combined to form a hedge.

Recommended

T. occidentalis (eastern white cedar) is a large, pyramidal tree with scale-like, evergreen needles. Many smaller and dwarf cultivars suitable for containers are available. **'Danica'** is a dwarf globe form growing about 18" tall and wide with bright emerald green foliage. **'Emerald'** is narrow and upright and is considered one of the hardiest cultivars, more so if it doesn't dry out in winter. It grows about 10' tall and 36" wide before it needs transplanting to a garden. **'Teddy'** is a dwarf, rounded to oval plant that grows 12–18" tall and 24" wide, with fine, feathery, blue-green foliage that tinges bronze in winter.

T. plicata (western red cedar) has a few dwarf cultivars small enough for containers. The species and its cultivars are hardy only to zone 5. **'Cuprea'** is a low, mound-forming cultivar with bright yellow-tipped, bronzy green foliage. It grows about 36" tall and wide. **'Pygmaea'** has dark, blue-tinged foliage and grows 24–36" tall and 12–24" wide. **'Stoneham Gold'** grows about 6' tall and 36" wide. New growth emerges bright yellow and matures to dark green. **'Whipcord'** has long, pendulous, rope-like foliage that gives the plant a mop-like appearance. It grows about 36" tall and spreads about 30".

T. occidentalis cultivar (above)
T. occidentalis 'Danica' (below)

Asparagus Fern
Asparagus

A. densiflorus 'Sprengeri' with begonias

One of the great plants for container gardening, asparagus fern provides a dense green base for taller plants. Not a true fern but more closely related to the vegetable, asparagus fern forms a dense root system and is ruggedly hardy if neglected.

Growing
Asparagus fern grows best in **light shade** or **partial shade** with protection from the afternoon sun. Avoid deep shade and direct sunlight. The potting mix should be kept evenly **moist** but allowed to dry out between waterings. Fertilize weekly during the growing season with quarter- to half-strength fertilizer. It must be overwintered indoors or thrown away at the end of the season.

Tips
Vigorous growth makes asparagus fern a good filler plant for mixed containers; its unique appearance and habit add an interesting visual element to any combination. It can also serve as a spiller, draping over the edge of a planter.

Recommended
A. densiflorus is an arching, tender perennial with light green, feathery, leaf-like stems. Two cultivars are commonly available. '**Myersii**' (foxtail fern) produces dense, foxtail-like stems that are 12–18" long. '**Sprengeri**' (emerald fern) has bright green, arching to drooping stems and a loose, open habit. It spreads 3–5' and is often grown where it will have room to hang.

Features: fern-like habit; bright green, needle-like or narrow, leaf-like stems; inconspicuous flowers; inedible, red berries **Height:** 12–36" **Spread:** 1–5' **Hardiness:** tender perennial grown as an annual **Grow rating:** easy

Bacopa
Sutera

S. cordata SNOWSTORM GIANT SNOWFLAKE with African daisy and fan flower

Bacopa can be lovely as a specimen in any raised pot, trailing to the deck or patio floor in a shower of white or lavender blooms. However, if you let it dry out, all the flowers will dry up, and the plant will take several weeks to rebound into flowering form.

Growing

Bacopa grows best in **partial shade** with protection from the hot afternoon sun. The potting mix should be **moist** and **well drained**. Don't allow this plant to completely dry out; the leaves will die quickly if they become dry. Cutting back dead growth may encourage new shoots to form.

Tips

A wonderful spiller, bacopa is a popular edge plant for hanging baskets, mixed containers and window boxes. It forms an attractive, spreading mound.

Recommended

S. cordata forms a dense, compact mound of heart-shaped leaves with scalloped edges and bears tiny, white, star-shaped flowers along its neat, trailing stems. **'Cabana Trailing Blue'** bears blue or purple flowers. **'Lavender Showers'** bears pale lavender flowers. **'Olympic Gold'** has gold variegated foliage with white flowers. SNOWSTORM GIANT SNOWFLAKE, from Proven Winners, is a vigorous plant with large, white flowers. SNOWSTORM PINK has light pink flowers.

Features: white, lavender, purple, blue or pink flowers; decorative foliage; trailing habit **Height:** 3–6" **Spread:** 12–24" **Hardiness:** tender perennial grown as an annual **Grow rating:** medium

Banana
Musa

M. basjoo with others

Tropical plants are the rage in summer garden schemes, none more than the dramatic form and colors of bananas. Forget the fruit; Midwest summers aren't long enough. Just enjoy the sculptural wonder of these tall, handsome accents.

Features: large, umbrella-like, evergreen foliage; rapid growth **Height:** 3–12'
Spread: 6–12' **Hardiness:** zones 8–10, but hardy to zone 6 with protection; tender bananas are hardy to 45° F but require a minimum temperature of 60° F to produce fruit
Grow rating: easy

Growing

Bananas grow best in **full sun** in the hottest part of your garden, but they will tolerate partial shade. The planting mix should be **fertile, moist, acidic** and **well drained**. Provide shelter from the wind because the leaves are prone to shredding. Fertilize weekly during the growing season with half-strength fertilizer. Mulch with compost.

Bananas can be grown as annuals or overwintered. Move plants to a sunny location indoors before the first frost. Keep the roots moist and reduce the fertilizer. Gradually move the plants into more and more sunlight in spring. Bananas grow rapidly and will need regular repotting if you overwinter them.

Alternately, allow the foliage to die with the first frosts, cut the plant back to 12–18", then dig up the corm and store it in a cool, dry location. The corm can be potted up spring and moved outdoors as the weather warms. Hardy bananas can be put outside after the risk of frost has passed. Tender bananas can be put outdoors in spring when night temperatures are around 60° F.

Tips

Bananas are excellent as specimens and focal points and are great in mixed containers. The large leaves will shade any plant beneath them, and in strong wind, they can act like sails on a boat, so make sure your container is properly weighted or tied down.

Recommended

M. basjoo (Japanese fiber banana) is the hardiest banana and can be perennial in the warmest parts of the Midwest. The fruit is edible but not palatable.

Basil
Ocimum

This sweetly scented culinary herb is perfectly at home on a sunny patio or deck just steps from the kitchen. Have it growing at waist height or above, and you'll be able to rub the leaves every time you pass the plant.

Growing

Basil grows best in a warm, sheltered location in **full sun**. The potting mix should be **moist** and **well drained**. Fertilize weekly with half-strength fertilizer. Pinch tips and remove flower spikes regularly to encourage bushy growth. Shelter containers in spring and fall when temperatures hover near freezing; basil is extremely sensitive to frost and will not revive if hit.

Tips

For a combination planter, consider three or more varieties—a miniature variety, a purple-leaved one and a traditional green type. Or, combine basil with other moisture-loving plants.

Recommended

O. basilicum is one of the most popular culinary herbs. There are dozens of varieties, including ones with large or tiny, green or purple, smooth or ruffled leaves, as well as varied flavors including anise, cinnamon and lemon. **'Green Globe'** forms a rounded mound of tiny leaves. **'Mammoth'** has huge leaves, up to 10" long and about half as wide. **'Purple Ruffles'** has dark purple leaves with frilly margins. **'Siam Queen'** is a cultivar of Thai basil with dark green foliage and dark purple flowers and stems.

O. basilicum 'Genovese' and *O. basilicum* 'Cinnamon'

Although basil will grow best in a warm spot outdoors, it can also be grown successfully in a bright window indoors to provide you with fresh leaves all year.

Features: bushy habit; fragrant, decorative leaves; pink, purple or white flowers **Height:** 12–24" **Spread:** 12–18" **Hardiness:** tender annual **Grow rating:** easy

Begonia
Begonia

B. x *tuberhybrida* cultivar with rubber plant, licorice plant, coleus, phormium and lamium

Mostly shade lovers, begonias come in anything from nearly flowerless rex species to enormous, multi-flowering 'Dragon Wing' varieties. Tuberous begonias, growing from a corm, need to rest after the garden season, but other types can double as houseplants after the outdoor container season. Whichever begonia you choose, you'll end up with a plant that does well in any container situation with little effort.

Growing

Begonias prefer **light shade** or **partial shade**, though wax begonias are quite sun tolerant. The potting mix should be **neutral to acidic, humus rich** and **well drained**. Mix some compost into a peat-based potting mix. Fertilize every two weeks with quarter- to half-strength fertilizer.

The tubers of tuberous begonias can be uprooted when the foliage dies back and stored in slightly moistened peat moss over winter. The tuber will sprout new

Features: bushy habit; decorative foliage; red, pink, orange, yellow, apricot or white, sometimes bicolored (picotee) flowers **Height:** 6–24" **Spread:** 6–24" **Hardiness:** tender perennial grown as an annual **Grow rating:** medium

shoots in late winter and can be potted for another season.

Tips

All begonias are useful for containers and planters on shaded patios, balconies, decks and porches. The trailing, tuberous varieties can be used in hanging baskets where the flowers can cascade over the edges.

Recommended

B. x *hybrida* '**Dragon Wing**' is a dramatic, large-leaved type with green foliage and large flowers. Two varieties are available: '**Dragon Wing Red**' and '**Dragon Wing Pink.**' Mature size is as large as 15" tall and 18" wide.

B. **Rex Cultorum hybrids** (rex begonias) are dense, mound-forming plants with dramatically patterned, high-contrast variegated foliage in shades of green, red, pink, white, bronze or purple. '**Escargot**' has spiraling, silver-striped, bronzy green leaves. '**Fire Flush**' has red-tinged, green and bronze variegated leaves. '**Fireworks**' has silvery white and purple-banded foliage. '**Wineuma**' has bright green leaves with scarlet undersides.

B. x *tuberhybrida* (tuberous begonias) form bushy mounds with green, bronze or purple foliage. The flowers can be held upright or in pendulous clusters. There are many hybrids of tuberous begonias available. **Non-stop Series** begonias are compact, bushy plants with red, yellow, apricot, orange, pink or white, double flowers. Two pendulous selections are '**Chanson,**' with single or semi-double flowers, and '**Illumination,**' with fully double flowers. Both have flowers in a wide range of colors.

B. hybrid (above), *B.* x *tuberhybrida* cultivar with phormium and others (below)

Black-Eyed Susan
Rudbeckia

R. hirta

As a cut flower, black-eyed Susan is long lasting in arrangements.

Features: summer through fall flowers in shades of yellow, orange, brown, red or gold, with brown or green centers **Height:** 18"–10' **Spread:** 12–36" **Hardiness:** zones 3–8; biennial or short-lived perennial grown as an annual **Grow rating:** easy

Understand the difference between your perennial garden favorite and the gloriosa daisy, which is grown as an annual and is far better adapted to containers. It packs great flower power on short, stocky plants and is perfect as a filler in combination containers.

Growing
Black-eyed Susan grows well in **full sun** or **partial shade**. The potting mix should be **well drained**. Water regularly,

though plants are fairly drought tolerant. Fertilize monthly with half-strength fertilizer. Pinch plants in June to encourage shorter, bushier growth. Deadhead to keep the plants neat, to encourage more flower production and to minimize self-seeding.

Tips

Perennial black-eyed Susan is good to use in themed containers such as wildflower or native containers because it isn't unruly and won't become floppy or messy, as some plants often do if grown in containers.

Recommended

R. hirta (gloriosa daisy) forms a bushy mound of bristly foliage and bears bright yellow, daisy-like flowers with brown centers from summer through to the first hard frost in fall. **'Becky'** is a dwarf cultivar that grows up to 12" tall and has large flowers in solid and multi-colored shades of yellow, orange, red or brown. **'Cherokee Sunset'** was a 2002 All-America Selections winner. It bears semi-double and double flowers in all colors. **'Irish Eyes'** bears bright yellow flowers with green centers. It grows 24–30" tall and is best in large containers where it will not look out of proportion. **Toto Series** are bushy, dwarf cultivars that grow 12–16" tall and bear single flowers with central brown cones with golden orange, lemon yellow or rich mahogany petals.

There are many more hybrids and species of black-eyed Susan. **R. fulgida var. sullivantii 'Goldsturm'** is a low maintenance, long-lived perennial that grows 24–30" tall and bears bright yellow, orange or red, brown-centered flowers. It is powdery mildew resistant. Other species grow 3–6' tall, making them less suitable for containers, though certainly worth a try.

R. hirta with dahlia, sedum, fan flower and sedge (above), *R. hirta* 'Irish Eyes' (below)

Black-Eyed Susan Vine
Thunbergia

T. alata (far left)

Black-eyed Susan vine is an alternative to morning glory as an annual vine. Petite flowers with brown centers mark this twiner. If you want it to climb, provide it with places to catch on a trellis, railing or obelisk.

Growing

Black-eyed Susan vine grows well in **full sun, partial shade** or **light shade**. The potting mix should be **moist** and **well drained** and have some organic matter such as earthworm castings or compost mixed in. Fertilize every two weeks during the growing season with quarter-strength fertilizer. It can be brought into the house over winter and then returned to the garden the following spring.

Tips

Black-eyed Susan vine is attractive trailing down from mixed containers and hanging baskets or climbing your decorative garden structures.

Recommended

T. alata is a vigorous, twining climber. It bears yellow flowers, often with dark centers, in summer and fall. **'African Sunset'** has flower colors that range from deep brick red to warm pastel colors to cream. **'Alba'** bears white flowers with dark purple-brown centers. **Suzie Hybrids** bear large flowers in yellow, orange or white.

Features: twining, evergreen vine; attractive foliage; yellow, orange, white or sometimes red, summer to fall flowers **Height:** 3–5' **Spread:** 1–5' **Hardiness:** tender perennial grown as an annual **Grow rating:** easy

Blood Grass
Imperata

Good manners and striking color are the two major assets of blood grass. This plant is non-invasive and won't overwhelm other plants.

Growing
Blood grass grows best in **full sun** or **partial shade**. The potting mix should be kept **moist** but not wet. Mix in compost or earthworm castings because this grass likes organic matter in its soil. Fertilize every two weeks during the growing season with quarter-strength fertilizer. Pull out any growth that doesn't turn red; green growth is more vigorous and will tend to dominate. Cover containers or move them to a sheltered location in winter.

Tips
Shoots emerge green with deep red tips, then mature to solid, blood red by the end of the season, creating a vertical element that works well with lower flowering plants or combined with other grasses.

Recommended
I. cylindrica **var.** *rubra* (*I. cylindrica* 'Red Baron') forms slow-spreading clumps of slender leaves. The grass blades emerge bright green tipped with red that spreads down the leaf as it matures, turning deep wine red by fall, then to copper in winter.

Blood grass is great for brightening up containers, adding color and texture offered by few other plants.

I. cylindrica var. *rubra* with sweet potato vine and spirea

Also called: Japanese blood grass
Features: perennial grass; colorful foliage; slender, upright habit **Height:** 12–18"
Spread: 12" **Hardiness:** zones 4–9
Grow rating: easy

Blueberry
Vaccinium

V. corymbosum 'Bluecrop'

Blueberries have an Achilles heel in many parts of the Midwest—their need for acidic soil—but that can be managed in a container. Their shallow roots like to be evenly moist but not saturated, so consider a drip irrigation system on a timer to provide the even watering cycle.

Features: bushy, deciduous to semi-evergreen shrub; mid-spring to early-summer flowers; tasty fruit; attractive foliage **Height:** 1–5' **Spread:** 2–5' **Hardiness:** zones 3–9 **Grow rating:** medium

Growing
Blueberries grow best in **full sun** but tolerate partial shade. The planting mix should be **peaty, acidic, moist** and **well drained**. Feed with quarter- to half-strength fertilizer in spring and after flowering. Blueberries are frost hardy. Very little pruning is required.

Tips
Dwarf blueberry shrubs can be placed on a patio or near an entranceway for easy harvesting, or in a spot that needs

some extra color in fall. Planting two different kinds (such as 'Bluecrop' and 'Blueray') together provides better cross-pollination and fruit production.

Recommended

V. corymbosum (highbush blueberry) is an upright, dense, well-branched shrub with medium to dark green summer foliage and outstanding orange to red, sometimes yellow, fall color. It produces hanging clusters of white, sometimes pink-tinged, flowers in late spring to early summer followed by spherical, blue-black fruit. **'Bluecrop'** is a drought-resistant plant whose tasty fruit ripens in mid-season. It grows 4–5' tall and wide. **'Blueray'** is a vigorous, upright shrub that grows 4–5' tall and wide. It bears light blue fruit and has red stems that stand out in winter. **'Sunshine Blue Dwarf'** is a dense, rounded shrub that grows 3–4' tall and wide and has shiny, silver-tinged green leaves that are semi-evergreen in the warmer south. It bears pink flowers in spring and is self-pollinating. It is hardy only to zone 5.

V. **Half-High Hybrids** are hybrids of *V. angustifolium* and *V. corymbosum*. Plants grow 18"–4' tall and 2–4' wide. The foliage is dark green with red fall color. Plants produce the best fruit when two varieties are near each other for cross-pollination. **'Northcountry'** is a partially self-pollinating variety that grows 18–24" tall and 3–4' wide and bears sky blue fruit. (Zones 3–7)

V. x **'Top Hat'** is a disease-resistant, dense, compact plant that grows 12–18" tall and wide. The glossy, dark green foliage turns bright red in fall. This shrub has abundant sweet, light blue fruit and does not need cross-pollination to bear fruit. (Zones 3–7)

Blue Fescue
Festuca

F. glauca ELIJAH BLUE with Swan River daisy and nemesia

Blue fescue's spiky form, blue color and restrained growth pattern make it an ideal selection for combining with many types of plants in containers.

Growing

Blue fescue grows well in **full sun** or **partial shade**. The potting mix should be **moist** and **well drained**. Fertilize once a month during the growing season with half-strength fertilizer. This grass is fairly drought tolerant, if you are prone to forgetting to water quite as often as you should. Trim back faded seedheads to keep the plants looking tidy. Move fescue containers to a sheltered location out of the wind and sun in winter. Cut it back in spring to revive it.

Tips

Use blue fescue as a mounding filler with taller plants or as the vertical element with low-growing or draping plants.

Recommended

F. filiformis (fine-leaf fescue) forms a low tuft of bright green, hair-like foliage. It grows 6–8" tall and spreads 8–12".

F. glauca (blue fescue) forms tidy, tufted clumps of fine, blue-toned foliage and produces short spikes of flowers in early summer. Cultivars and hybrids come in varying heights and in shades ranging from blue to olive green. ELIJAH BLUE, a Proven Selection by Proven Winners, and **'Boulder Blue'** have intense blue coloring. **'Skinner's Blue'** is one of the hardiest selections.

Features: tuft-forming, perennial grass; silvery or gray-blue to olive green or bright green foliage; spiky or relaxed habit **Height:** 6–12" **Spread:** 10–12" **Hardiness:** zones 3–8 **Grow rating:** easy

Caladium
Caladium

Color in shady nooks is a desire of many gardeners, and caladiums are a perfect choice because they come in a wide range of colors. The tropically inspired leaves are typically large and multi-hued.

Growing
Caladium prefers to grow in **partial to full shade**. The potting mix should be **moist, well drained, humus rich** and **slightly acidic**.

Dig up tubers in fall after the leaves die back. Remove as much potting mix as possible, let them dry for a few days and store them in slightly damp peat moss at 55–60° F. You can also simply bring the whole container inside over winter as is. Tubers can be divided in spring before planting. Divisions of tubers are more subject to fungal diseases because of the freshly exposed surfaces. Start tubers indoors in late winter to early spring. Make sure the knobby side of the tuber is facing up and is level with the soil surface or just under. Add a little bonemeal or fishmeal to the planting hole.

Tips
Caladiums look great as specimens or when mass planted. They enjoy the humidity near pools and can be placed under shade trees for extra color.

Recommended
C.* x *hortulanum (*C. bicolor*) is a complex group of hybrids with large, often tufted, arrow-shaped, dark green foliage that is variously marked and patterned with red, white, pink, green, rose, salmon, silver or bronze. Each leaf is 6–12" long.

C. x hortulanum with English ivy and impatiens

All parts of caladium may irritate the skin, and ingesting this plant will cause stomach upset.

Also called: elephant ears, heart-of-Jesus, mother-in-law plant, angel wings **Features:** ornate foliage; habit **Height:** 18–24" **Spread:** 18–24" **Hardiness:** tender perennial grown as an annual **Grow rating:** easy

Calla Lily
Zantedeschia

Z. elliottiana hybrid with pansies

Don't feel you must store all the rhizomes you lift in fall; these plants grow vigorously, and you may need only a few pieces for the following summer.

Features: clump-forming habit; glossy, green foliage; summer flowers **Height:** 16–36" **Spread:** 8–24" **Hardiness:** tender, rhizomatous perennial grown as an annual **Grow rating:** medium

*I*f you equate calla lilies to white, you're missing an opportunity to inject great color in your containers with unequaled, upward-facing flowers.

Growing
Calla lilies grow best in **full sun** in a sheltered location. The potting mix should be **moist** and **well drained** until the leaves begin to unfurl. Once plants are actively growing, the soil can be kept quite wet. The potato-like tubers need to

be planted with "eyes" slightly above the soil line, and they will need to be watered regularly. Fertilize every two weeks with quarter- to half-strength fertilizer. Deadhead the faded flowers and stems.

Slowly reduce the water toward the end of summer to encourage dormancy and the foliage to die back. After a light frost, remove the foliage and stems from the rhizome, being careful not to damage it. Wash the rhizome gently under tepid water, removing soil and debris. Dust the rhizome with a fungicide and leave it to dry for a week at room temperature in a well-ventilated room. Once cured, store the rhizome in a paper bag in a cool, dark location at 41–50° F until it's time to plant it again in spring.

Tips
Calla lilies are stunning additions to large, colorful mixed or specimen containers. Try a theme garden with a combination of water-loving plants such as elephant ears, rush and sweet flag.

Recommended
Z. aethiopica forms a clump of glossy, green, arrow-shaped leaves. Ornamental, white spathes surround the creamy yellow flower spikes. Cultivars and hybrids are available.

Z. elliottiana (yellow calla, golden calla) forms a clump of white-spotted, dark green, heart-shaped leaves. Yellow spathes surround bright yellow flower spikes. This species is the parent plant of many popular hybrids.

Z. rehmannii (pink arum, pink calla) forms a clump of narrow, dark green leaves. White, pink or purple spathes surround yellow flower spikes. This species is also the parent of many hybrids.

Z. elliottiana hybrid with petunia, canna lily, dracaena and Swan River daisy (above)
Z. elliottiana hybrid (below)

Canna Lily
Canna

C. hybrid with lobelia

Canna lilies are dramatic, tropical-looking plants with flower spikes on top of interesting foliage. Most are too tall for normal containers, so be sure to select a dwarf variety or plan for a six-foot-plus stalk. They grow from a rhizomatous tuber and form many more by season's end.

Growing
Canna lilies grow best in **full sun**. The potting mix should be **moist** and **well drained**. Fertilize every two weeks with quarter- to half-strength fertilizer. Deadhead regularly to prolong blooming. Once all of the buds have opened and the flowers are finished, remove the stalk down to the next side shoot.

When planting, lay the rhizomes flat and just barely cover them with soil. Transplant canna lilies earlier than June to ensure they will flower before the end of the season.

Tips
The silvery foliage of dusty miller and licorice plant creates an excellent backdrop for the colorful foliage and flowers of canna lily.

Recommended
A wide range of canna lilies are available, including cultivars and hybrids with green, bronze, purple or yellow-and-green-striped foliage. Flowers may be white, red, orange, pink, yellow or sometimes bicolored. **Pfitzer Series** has dwarf selections that grow about 36" tall.

Pairing coleus with canna lily gives a container a bold, tropical look.

Features: green, blue-green, bronze, purple, yellow or sometimes variegated foliage; red, white, orange, pink, yellow or sometimes bicolored flowers **Height:** 3–7' **Spread:** 18–36" **Hardiness:** zones 7–11; tender, rhizomatous perennial grown as an annual **Grow rating:** medium

Clematis
Clematis

C. integrifolia

lematis is a perennial vine that used to prove a real challenge for a container grower. Luckily, recent breeding has developed several lines of plants just for containers. Look for the Patio Collection, bred by Englishman Raymond J. Evison.

Growing

Clematis plants prefer **full sun** but tolerate full shade. Try to keep the container shaded because these plants do best when their roots stay cool. The potting mix should be **moist** and **well drained** and have some compost mixed in. Fertilize every two weeks during the growing season with quarter- to half-strength fertilizer.

Features: twining vine or bushy perennial; attractive, leafy habit; flowers in shades of blue, purple, pink, white, yellow or red or sometimes bicolored **Height:** 1–5'
Spread: 1–4' **Hardiness:** zones 3–8
Grow rating: medium

These hardy plants have sensitive roots. Freezing and thawing will more likely kill your clematis vine than extreme cold. Move the container to a location where the temperature will stay fairly even, such as a protected patio or porch or an unheated garage or shed.

Tips

Clematis plants make a lovely addition to a mixed container where you can grow them up an obelisk or trellis, or let them spill over the edge. The abundant flowers make these plants worth including in your containers, even if they survive only a few years.

Recommended

C. alpina (alpine clematis) is a twining vine that blooms in spring and early summer, bearing bell-shaped, blue flowers with white centers.

C. integrifolia (solitary clematis) is a bushy perennial, rather than a climbing vine, though it has flexible, trailing growth that can be trained to grow up a low trellis or spill over the edge of a container. It bears flared, bell-shaped, purple flowers in summer.

C. x jackmanii (Jackman clematis) is a twining vine that bears large, purple flowers in summer. Many hybrids are available, with flowers in a wide range of colors.

C. viticella RAYMOND EVISON PATIO CLEMATIS COLLECTION are slow-growing, twining, compact vines that grow 3–4' tall and 18–36" wide and are hardy to zone 4. The cultivars **'Angelique,' 'Parisienne,' 'Chantilly,' 'Cezanne,' 'Picardy,' 'Versailles'** and **'Bourbon'** bloom well into fall in varied shades of magenta, purple and purple-blue.

C. x jackmanii (above), *C. integrifolia* (below)

Clover

Trifolium

Because of its small stature, clover can be lost to the eye when mixed with other plants in beds but seems to stand out when planted in containers, both as a specimen or when mixed with other annuals.

Growing

Clover is best grown in **full sun** or **partial shade**. The potting mix should be **moist, well drained** and **neutral**. Fertilize once during the growing season, about a month after you plant it out, with half-strength fertilizer. Move it to a sheltered location in winter, or throw it away after the first frost and plant new clover the following summer.

Tips

This lovely little plant will add interest to mixed containers. It is especially striking when grouped with other plants with dramatically colored foliage or bright, contrasting flowers.

Recommended

T. repens is a low, spreading perennial that is often grown as an annual. It is rarely grown in favor of the many attractive cultivars. The small, rounded flower clusters can be pink, red, yellow or white. **'Dark Dancer'** ('Atropurpureum') has a dwarf habit and dark burgundy leaves with lime green margins. **'Salsa Dancer'** produces bright green foliage with burgundy and white markings in the center of each leaf and bears white flowers.

Because of its invasive nature, clover is ideally suited to container culture.

T. repens 'Dark Dancer' with coleus and others

Features: spreading habit; decorative, often variegated foliage; small, globe-shaped, white, pink, red or yellow flowers **Height:** 3–12" **Spread:** 12–18" or more **Hardiness:** zones 4–8; perennial grown as an annual **Grow rating:** easy

Coleus

Solenostemon (Coleus)

S. scutellarioides SEDONA

Growing

Coleus prefers to grow in **light shade** or **partial shade** but tolerates full shade if not too dense and full sun if the plants are watered regularly. The potting mix should be **humus rich, moist** and **well drained**. Mix in some compost or earthworm castings. When flower buds develop, it is best to pinch them off because the plants tend to stretch out and become less attractive after they flower.

These plants are perennials that are grown as annuals, but they also make attractive houseplants. Cuttings taken from favorites in late summer can be grown indoors in a bright room by a sunny window.

Tips

The bold, colorful foliage creates a dramatic display when several different selections are grouped together in a single container or group of containers. Coleus also makes an excellent accent plant in a mixed container with other annuals or perennials.

Recommended

S. scutellarioides (*Coleus blumei* var. *verschaffeltii*) cultivars and hybrids form bushy mounds of foliage. The leaf edges range from slightly toothed to very ruffled. The leaves are usually multi-colored with shades ranging from pale greenish yellow to deep purple-black. Plants grow

Coleus has always been available in a great range of colors, and it is only more desirable as new varieties emerge onto the market in colors such as plum, burgundy, chartreuse, gold, lime, copper, wine and almost black.

Features: bushy habit; colorful, often variegated foliage in shades of green, yellow, pink, red, burgundy or purple **Height:** 6–36" **Spread:** 6–24" **Hardiness:** tender perennial grown as an annual **Grow rating:** easy

6–36" tall, depending on the cultivar, and the spread is usually equal to the height. Some interesting cultivars include '**Black Prince**,' with deep purple, almost black foliage; '**Fishnet Stockings**,' with purple-veined, bright green foliage; '**Merlin's Magic**,' with deeply divided, slightly ruffled, purple, pink, burgundy or yellow and green variegated foliage; and SEDONA, a Proven Selection by Proven Winners, with pink-veined, orange foliage.

Coleus can be trained to grow into a tree form. Pinch off the lower leaves and side branches as they grow to create a long, bare stem with leaves on only the upper half. Once the plant reaches the desired height, pinch from the top to create a bushy, rounded crown.

S. scutellarioides cultivar with begonia and fig (above)
S. scutellarioides cultivar with coral bells and others (below)

Coral Bells

Heuchera

H. AMBER WAVES, alone and with African daisy, in front of sedge (above), *H.* hybrid with sweet potato vine, begonia and sweet flag (below)

Also called: heuchera, alum root **Features:** mound-forming or spreading perennial; scalloped or heart-shaped, colorful foliage; red, pink, purple, white or yellow, small, summer flowers **Height:** 1–4' **Spread:** 12–18" **Hardiness:** zones 3–8 **Grow rating:** easy

From soft yellow-greens and oranges to midnight purples and silvery, dappled maroons, coral bells offer a great variety of foliage colors with striking leaf shapes.

Growing

Coral bells grow best in **light shade** or **partial shade**. Foliage colors can bleach out in full sun. The potting mix should be **neutral to alkaline, moist** and **well drained**. Mix in some compost or earthworm castings. Fertilize once a month during the growing season with quarter- to half-strength fertilizer. Cover them or move them to a sheltered location in winter. Trim back faded flower stalks in spring.

Tips

Coral bells are attractive fillers in mixed containers, where the colorful foliage contrasts particularly well with grasses, ferns and yellow-flowered plants such as lady's mantle, iris and dahlia. Combine different selections of coral bells for an interesting display.

Recommended

There are many hybrids and cultivars of coral bells available. The following are just a few of the possibilities. **'Caramel'** has apricot-colored foliage and pink flowers. **'Chocolate Ruffles'** has ruffled, glossy, brown foliage with purple undersides that give the leaves a bronzed appearance. **'Coral Cloud'** forms a clump of glossy, crinkled leaves and bears pinkish red flowers. **'Firefly'** develops a clump of dark green leaves with attractive, fragrant, bright pinkish red flowers. Both **'Lime Rickey'** and DOLCE KEY LIME PIE, from Proven Winners, form a low mass of chartreuse leaves. **'Marmalade'** has foliage that emerges red and matures to orange-yellow. **'Montrose Ruby'** has bronzy purple foliage with bright red undersides. **'Northern Fire'** has red flowers and leaves mottled with silver. **'Obsidian'** has lustrous, dark purple, nearly black, foliage. **'Pewter Veil'** has silvery purple leaves with dark gray veins. Its flowers are white flushed with pink. **'Velvet Night'** has dark purple leaves with a metallic sheen and creamy white flowers.

Coral bells are delicate-looking woodland plants and can be combined with other woodland plants such as ferns to create a themed container.

H. DOLCE KEY LIME PIE **with sedge and African daisy**

Croton

Codiaeum

C. variegatum var. pictum

All parts are poisonous if ingested, and repeated contact with sap may irritate skin.

Features: bushy habit; colorful, patterned foliage **Height:** 12–36" **Spread:** 12–18" **Hardiness:** tender perennial grown as an annual **Grow rating:** easy

This beauty takes on shrub-size proportions in warm climates. Croton's leaves are stunning in a range of fiery colors.

Growing

Croton grows best in **full sun** and prefers a humid environment to a dry one. The planting mix should be **moist, humus rich** and **well drained**. Fertilize once or twice a month during the growing season with half-strength fertilizer. Keep plants bushy by cutting the stem back to a joining leaf.

If you plan to overwinter croton, you will need to bring it inside before night temperatures drop below 50° F. Allow the planting mix to dry slightly between watering during winter.

Plants may experience some leaf drop when moved. Younger plants are less subject to moving shock. Repot when necessary. If plants become too large, cut them back by one-third in early spring and use some of the cuttings to start new plants.

Tips

Croton is a great plant to add to tropical-themed containers. Use it as a thriller in a combination container, and give it room to spread out.

Recommended

C. variegatum **var.** *pictum* is a bushy, upright, woody-based perennial that bears leaves in a variety of shapes including narrow, oval, lobed and forked. Some cultivars have leaves that twist, spiral or constrict. The leaf colors range from red to yellow to green and everything in between, in a variety of patterns. The fluffy, cream-colored flowers are rarely produced in pots.

Cuphea
Cuphea

Several good container plants are members of the genus *Cuphea*, including Mexican heather and cigar flower. The small, tubular blooms are attractive to both hummingbirds and butterflies. Some varieties can get boisterous in a mixed container but respond well to drastic pruning.

Growing

Cupheas grow well in **full sun** or **partial shade**. The potting mix should be **moist** and **well drained**. Short periods of drought are tolerated. Fertilize monthly during the growing season with half-strength fertilizer. These plants are tender and can be treated like annuals or brought indoors at the end of summer and treated like houseplants.

Tips

Cupheas are excellent plants for containers. The ever-expanding number of species and range of flower colors available allows a good choice between complementary and contrasting colors.

Recommended

C. hybrids offer a differing selection from the species and cultivars in subtle ways, including flower color and habit. The FLAMENCO SERIES are Proven Selections from Proven Winners. FLAMENCO TANGO has bright purple-pink flowers. FLAMENCO RUMBA bears fiery red flowers with dark purple centers.

C. hyssopifolia (Mexican heather, false heather, elfin herb) is a bushy, branching plant that forms a flat-topped mound. The flowers have green calyces and light purple, pink or sometimes white petals. The plants bloom from summer to frost. **'Allyson Purple'** ('Allyson') is a dwarf

plant that bears lavender flowers. **'Desert Snow'** has white flowers.

C. ignea (*C. platycentra*; cigar flower, firecracker plant) is a spreading, freely branching plant. Thin, tubular, bright red flowers are produced from late spring to frost. It can also be used as a houseplant.

Features: red, pink, purple, violet, green or white flowers **Height:** 6–24" **Spread:** 10–36" **Hardiness:** tender shrub grown as an annual **Grow rating:** medium

Dahlia

Dahlia

D. hybrid with zinnia, nasturtium and thyme

Dahlia cultivars span a vast array of colors, sizes and flower forms, but breeders have yet to develop true blue, scented and frost-hardy varieties.

Features: bushy habit; attractive foliage; summer flowers in shades of red, yellow, orange, pink, purple, white or sometimes bicolored **Height:** 8"–5' **Spread:** 8–24" **Hardiness:** tender, tuberous perennial grown as an annual **Grow rating:** medium

Breadth of size, shape and colors mark the dahlias, but beware the mature size of those varieties you select for a container. Look for the shorter varieties that come into bloom sooner than their large-flowering relatives.

Growing

Dahlias prefer **full sun**. The potting mix should be **humus rich, moist** and **well drained**. Fertilize every two weeks with quarter-strength fertilizer. Deadhead to keep plants neat and to encourage more blooms.

Dahlias are tender, tuberous perennials that are treated as annuals. The tubers can be lifted in fall and stored over winter in slightly moist peat moss. Pot them and keep them in a bright room when they start sprouting in mid- to late winter.

Tips

Dahlias make attractive, colorful additions to mixed containers. Their sturdy, bushy growth gives them a shrubby appearance that can be used to visually anchor a mixed container that includes softer-looking or trailing plants. The stunning flowers draw the eye and create a strong focal point, so use them in places you want people to see or notice.

Recommended

D. **hybrids** are bushy, tuberous perennials with glossy leaves in shades of green, bronze or purple. They are generally described by their flower shape, such as collarette, decorative or peony-flowered. The flowers range in size from 2–12" and are available in shades of purple, pink, white, yellow, orange, red or bicolored. **'Amazon Pink and Rose'** is a miniature plant with yellow-centered, pink, semi-double flowers. The petals are light pink with deep pink bases. **'Bishop of Llandaff'** has dark red, semi-double flowers and bronze foliage. **'Dalstar Yellow'** is a miniature plant with pale yellow, semi-double flowers. **'Dalina Mini Bahamas'** is a dwarf plant with glossy, green foliage and fuchsia pink, double flowers. **'David Howard'** has multi-tonal orange, double flowers that contrast strikingly with its dark purple foliage. **'Figaro'** can be started from seed and has double and semi-double flowers in a wide range of colors.

D. 'Chic' (above), *D.* hybrids with lobelia and dracaena (below)

Daylily
Hemerocallis

H. fulva 'Flore Pleno'

More than 12,000 daylily selections have been developed, with sometimes hundreds more added yearly.

Features: clump-forming perennial; spring and summer flowers in every color except blue and pure white; grass-like foliage
Height: 1–4' **Spread:** 1–4' **Hardiness:** zones 2–9 **Grow rating:** easy

The daylily's adaptability and durability, combined with its variety in color, blooming period, size and texture, explain this perennial's enduring popularity. If you're not a fan of its strap-like leaves, plant it in the rear of a mixed container.

Growing
Daylilies grow in any light from **full sun to full shade**. The deeper the shade, the fewer flowers will be produced. The potting mix should be **moist** and **well drained**, but these plants will tolerate both wet and dry conditions. Fertilize monthly during the growing season with half-strength fertilizer. Deadhead to encourage more flowering. Move containers to a sheltered location in winter.

Tips
Plant daylilies alone, or group them in containers. Although the small selections seem best suited to container culture, the larger plants make a bold statement and will grow equally well in containers.

Recommended
Daylilies come in an almost infinite number of sizes and colors over the range of species, cultivars and hybrids. They all form clumps of strap-like foliage and produce a cluster of buds on a stem that is held above the foliage. The buds open one at a time, and each lasts for a single day.

Diascia
Diascia

One can never have enough floriferous container plants, and diascia qualifies mightily for this role. The plants are less than a foot tall and spreading, often draping over the rim of a pot or window box.

Growing
Diascias prefer **full sun**. The potting mix should be **moist** and **well drained**. Fertilize weekly with quarter- to half-strength fertilizer. Deadhead regularly, and pinch plant tips to increase bushiness. If flowering becomes sparse or flowers fade in the summer heat, shearing will encourage a fresh flush of blooms in a few weeks when the weather cools.

Tips
Diascia can do double duty in your container as both a filler and a spiller. The flower colors are easy to mix with many different annual species.

Recommended
D. FLYING COLORS SERIES from Proven Winners grow 8–12" tall, are very heat and frost tolerant and have large, early-blooming flowers. 'Apricot' has apricot flowers and dense, dark green foliage. 'Coral' has bright coral flowers. 'Trailing Antique Rose' has a trailing habit and bears deep rose flowers.

D. Whisper™ **Series** from Simply Beautiful are semi-trailing, spreading plants 10–15" tall that bloom in shades of pink and red.

Diascias are generally frost hardy and bloom well into fall. They can be planted out in early April, and when hardened off, they withstand frosts and even a light freeze.

D. FLYING COLORS SERIES 'Trailing Antique Rose'

Also called: twinspur **Features:** bushy, spreading habit; interesting, tiny flowers in shades of pink, red, coral and apricot **Height:** 8–16" **Spread:** 18–20" **Hardiness:** zones 8–10; tender perennial grown as an annual **Grow rating:** medium

Dichondra
Dichondra

D. argentea 'Silver Falls'

The natural, super-cascading habit and vigorous, silvery growth of 'Silver Falls' dichondra combine to act as a true spiller, with a neutral hue that complements almost any flower color in a container. It will continue its downward growth, so some tip pruning may be needed.

Growing

'Silver Falls' dichondra grows best in **full sun**. The potting mix should be **moist** and **well drained**, but the plant tolerates drought and recovers quickly from a wilted condition. It also tolerates hot, humid summers. Feed plants monthly with quarter- to half-strength fertilizer. If starting from seed, sow indoors 12 weeks before the last spring frost.

Tips

'Silver Falls' dichondra can be used to accent mixed containers and is beautiful as a hanging basket specimen. The silver foliage looks wonderful when trailing over rock walls and raised beds.

Recommended

D. argentea **'Silver Falls'** bears thick, soft-textured, fan-shaped, silver foliage on silver stems. The plant branches very well without any pinching. The flowers are pale green and inconspicuous. The plant may self-seed during the growing season or root where the stems touch the ground. **'Emerald Falls'** has deep green foliage and a dense, symmetrical habit that is slightly larger in spread.

Also called: kidneyweed, silver ponyfoot
Features: trailing habit; attractive, silvery foliage **Height:** 2–3" **Spread:** 3–4'; may trail more in southern parts of the Midwest **Hardiness:** zones 9–10; perennial grown as an annual **Grow rating:** easy

Dusty Miller

Senecio

S. cineraria 'Silver Dust'

usty miller is an old standby of the annual garden, and its soft, silvery gray, deeply lobed foliage works equally well in containers. It creates a good backdrop to show off the brightly colored flowers or foliage of other plants.

Growing

Dusty miller prefers **full sun** but tolerates light shade. The potting mix should be **well drained**. Fertilize no more than once a month during the growing season with quarter-strength fertilizer. Pinch off the flowers before they bloom; the flowers aren't showy and steal energy that would otherwise go to the foliage. It can survive winter in a sheltered location in many parts of the Midwest.

Tips

The soft, silvery, lacy leaves of dusty miller are its main feature, and it is used primarily as a contrast or backdrop plant.

Recommended

S. cineraria forms a mound of fuzzy, silvery gray, lobed or finely divided foliage. Many cultivars have been developed. **'Cirrus'** has lobed, silvery green or white foliage. **'Silver Dust'** has deeply lobed, silvery white foliage. **'Silver Lace'** has delicate, silvery white foliage that glows in the moonlight.

Features: bushy habit; variably lobed foliage in shades of silvery gray **Height:** 12–24"
Spread: equal to height or slightly narrower
Hardiness: semi-tender annual
Grow rating: easy

Dwarf Morning Glory
Convolvulus

C. tricolor

Morning glory can be a bit robust for most containers, but a similar flowered plant, dwarf morning glory, grows in a mound and won't need a trellis to climb over.

Growing

Dwarf morning glory prefers **full sun**. The potting mix must be **well drained**. Fertilize no more than once, about a month after planting, with quarter-strength fertilizer. This plant will produce lots of foliage but few flowers in soil that is too fertile.

Tips

Dwarf morning glory is a compact, mounding plant that can be grown in containers and hanging baskets. It makes a nice plant to grow alone in a small container and also mixes well with other annuals. The mounding to slightly trailing form looks good when combined with grasses.

Recommended

C. tricolor is a compact, mound-forming plant that bears trumpet-shaped flowers that last only a single day, opening in the morning and twisting shut that evening. **Ensign Series** has low-growing, spreading plants that grow about 6" tall. **'Royal Ensign'** has deep blue flowers with white and yellow throats. **'Star of Yalta'** bears deep purple flowers that pale to violet in the throat.

Although this plant is related to the noxious weed C. arvensis (field bindweed), dwarf morning glory is in no way invasive or problematic.

Features: mound-forming habit; blue, purple or pink, summer flowers sometimes variegated with yellow and white throats **Height:** 6–16"
Spread: 10–12" **Hardiness:** annual
Grow rating: medium

Elder

Sambucus

S. *nigra* BLACK BEAUTY with African daisy, coral bells and euphorbia (above), S. *nigra* BLACK LACE (below)

The native elder shrub has been transformed into lacy, small plants that add textural punch to combination planters. Most bloom in early summer and set fruit like their native counterpart, and birds appreciate the berries.

Growing

Elders grow well in **full sun** or **partial shade**. Yellow-leaved cultivars and varieties develop the best color in light shade or partial shade, and black-, burgundy- or purple-leaved cultivars develop the best color in full sun. The potting mix should be **moist** and **well drained**. Fertilize monthly during summer with quarter-strength fertilizer. Stop fertilizing before fall to give

Features: large, bushy, deciduous shrub; early-summer flowers; edible fruit; colorful, decorative foliage **Height:** 2–10' in containers **Spread:** 2–10' in containers **Hardiness:** zones 3–8 **Grow rating:** medium

S. nigra 'Madonna' (above)
S. racemosa 'Goldilocks' (center)

S. nigra BLACK BEAUTY (below)

the plant time to harden off for winter. Move containers to a sheltered location for winter or cover them to protect them from winds and temperature fluctuations.

Prune plants back in spring to keep them at a suitable size. You may have to root prune them every few years or move them to a garden when they become too large for the container.

Tips
Elders make a strong architectural statement and are best suited to large containers. Train them as small, single- or multi-stemmed trees. Plant annuals with contrasting flower colors around the base of an elder for an eye-catching combination.

Recommended
S. canadensis (American elder), *S. nigra* (black elder) and *S. racemosa* (European red elder) are rounded shrubs with white or pink flowers followed by red or dark purple berries. Cultivars are available with green, yellow, bronze or purple foliage and deeply divided or feathery foliage. *S. canadensis* '**Lanciniata**' has lacy, green foliage that gives this shrub a fern-like or feathery appearance. *S. nigra* BLACK BEAUTY, a Proven Winners Color Choice Selection, has dark purple, almost black, foliage that darkens as summer progresses. *S. nigra* BLACK LACE, another Proven Winners Color Choice Selection, produces finely cut, black foliage and pink flowers. *S. nigra* '**Madonna**' bears dark green foliage with wide, irregular, yellow margins. *S. racemosa* '**Sutherland Gold**' has deeply divided, yellow-green foliage.

Elderberries will attract birds to your garden.

Elephant Ears
Alocasia, Colocasia, Xanthosoma

C. esculenta with coleus, sweet potato vine and others

Huge leaves with a definite tropical look are the hallmarks of elephant ears. Grown from large tubers, these moisture-loving foliage plants tower above most elements in a combination container.

Growing

Elephant ears grow well in **partial to light shade** and may tolerate full shade. The potting mix should be **humus rich,**

C. esculenta is often included in water gardens and can actually be grown in up to 8" of water. Try it in a large water barrel if you want something other than miniature water lilies.

Features: tuberous or rhizomatous; large, attractive leaves **Height:** 2–4' **Spread:** 2–4' **Hardiness:** tender perennial grown as an annual **Grow rating:** medium

slightly acidic and moist. Fertilize every two weeks during the growing season with quarter-strength fertilizer. Move elephant ears indoors before winter, or store the tuberous or rhizomatous roots in a cool, dry location until spring.

Tips

Planted alone in a moist container or combined with other moisture-lovers, these plants make a striking addition to any container garden.

Recommended

A. sanderiana (kris plant) has thick, erect stems and silver-tinted, dark green leaves with scalloped edges and purple undersides. Insignificant, arum-like flowers may emerge. All parts are very poisonous if ingested. Keep away from children and pets.

C. esculenta (taro) is a tuberous, warm-climate plant that produces a clump of large, green, heart-shaped leaves. Cultivars with red- or purple-veined to dark purple or bronze foliage are available. 'Black Magic' has dark purple leaves. 'Fontanesii' has green leaves with red to purple stems, veins and margins.

C. esculenta 'Illustris' (above), *A. macrorrhiza* with begonia and coleus (below)

X. violaceum (blue taro) is a large, tuberous perennial with large, arrow-shaped foliage and purple leaf stalks. It has creamy white veins on the upper leaf surface and violet purple veins at the leaf margins and on the leaf undersides.

These plants can withstand heavy insect infestations before showing any symptoms that require treatment.

English Ivy
Hedera

nglish ivy has three strong attributes in a container: it spills beautifully; its dense foliage gives it a lush green look; and it thrives in almost any light conditions. If allowed, it will root in garden soil and continue its rapid growth pattern, but it does not mind frequent pruning.

Growing

English ivy prefers **light shade** or **partial shade** but will adapt to any light conditions from full sun to full shade. The potting mix should be **moist** and **well drained**. Fertilize every two weeks with quarter- to half-strength fertilizer. Although there are several hardy selections, the most decorative English ivy selections are not hardy and may not survive winter.

Tips

English ivy is a pretty, fast-growing vine. It quickly fills in the spaces between other plants in a mixed container or hanging basket.

Recommended

H. helix is a vigorous vine with glossy, dark green leaves. A number of cultivars have been developed for outdoor cultivation, so check the vine section of your local garden center. Many interesting varieties are grown as houseplants, and these are the ones to include in mixed containers. 'Calico' has green, gray and cream mottled foliage. 'Flamenco' has small, frilly, dark green, glossy leaves. 'Maple Leaf' has deeply lobed, star-like, dark green leaves.

H. helix with phormium and maidenhair vine

Features: evergreen or semi-evergreen climbing vine or groundcover; decorative foliage **Height:** 1–10' in containers **Spread:** 1–10' in containers **Hardiness:** zones 5–10; tender vine grown as an annual **Grow rating:** easy

Euonymus
Euonymus

E. fortunei GOLD SPLASH

These variable shrubs include some of the best-suited woody plants for container culture. Because they are woody plants, they may overwhelm smaller, more tender annuals or perennials in a mixed planter.

Features: deciduous or evergreen shrub, small tree, groundcover or climber; decorative foliage; good fall color **Height:** 18"–5'
Spread: 2–5' **Hardiness:** zones 5–9 **Grow rating:** medium

Growing

Euonymus prefers **full sun** but tolerates light shade or partial shade. The potting mix should be **moist** and **well drained**. Fertilize monthly during the growing season with quarter-strength fertilizer. Move this plant to a sheltered location out of the wind and sun in winter.

Wintercreeper cultivars are vigorous, spreading plants that can be trimmed as required to keep them within the desired growing area. They tolerate severe pruning.

Tips

Wintercreeper can be pruned to a mounded shape for a filler or into an upright shrub as an alternative for boxwood, kept low and wide as a spiller or used as a vine on a trellis.

Recommended

E. fortunei (wintercreeper euonymus) is rarely grown in favor of the wide and attractive variety of cultivars. These can be prostrate, climbing or mounding evergreens, often with attractive, variegated foliage. BLONDY ('Interbolwji') has yellow foliage with narrow, irregular, dark green margins. **'Emerald Gaiety'** is a vigorous shrub that sends out long shoots that will attempt to scale any nearby surface. The foliage is bright green with irregular, creamy margins that turn pink in winter. **'Emerald 'n' Gold'** is a bushy selection that has green leaves with wide, gold margins. The foliage turns pinky red during winter and spring.

Euphorbia
Euphorbia

E. polychroma (above), *E.* 'Diamond Frost' (below)

Euphorbia is a neat, rounded perennial, typically with yellow flowers and good fall color, which is well suited to low-maintenance and drought-tolerant containers.

Features: mound-forming habit; yellow to green, spring to mid-summer flowers; decorative foliage; fall color **Height:** 12–24" **Spread:** 12–24" **Hardiness:** zones 4–8; tender perennial grown as an annual **Grow rating:** easy

E. dulcis 'Chameleon' (above), *E.* 'Diamond Frost' (below)

Growing

Euphorbia grows well in **full sun** or **light shade**. The potting mix should be **humus rich, moist** and **well drained**. This plant is drought tolerant. Fertilize once during the growing season, preferably just after flowering is complete, with quarter- to half-strength fertilizer. Move containers to a sheltered location protected from temperature fluctuations in winter.

Tips

Look for 'Diamond Frost,' a tender perennial grown as an annual. It can be grown singly in a pot to form a white ball of bloom or used as a filler with taller, more robust flowering plants.

Recommended

E. **'Diamond Frost'** is an award-winning, tender perennial from Proven Winners that is grown as an annual. It is covered with tiny white flowers all summer long, is self-cleaning (no deadheading) and is tolerant of drought and heat.

E. dulcis (sweet spurge) is a compact, upright perennial. The spring flowers and bracts are yellow-green. The dark bronzy green leaves turn red or orange in fall. **'Chameleon'** has purple-red foliage that turns darker purple in fall.

E. griffithii **'Fireglow'** has light green leaves, orange stems and bright orange bracts. **'Fire Charm'** is a more compact selection.

E. polychroma (*E. epithymoides*; cushion spurge) is a mounding, clump-forming perennial. Long-lasting, yellow bracts surround the inconspicuous flowers. The foliage turns shades of purple, red or orange in fall. There are several cultivars available. **'Candy'** has purple-tinged leaves and stems.

Fan Flower

Scaevola

Fan flower's intriguing, one-sided flowers add interest to hanging baskets, planters and window boxes. It requires a fair amount of maintenance to keep it in flower—don't neglect watering, fertilize regularly and trim it back to keep it bushy. Its beautiful flower clusters are worth the effort.

Growing

Fan flower grows well in **full sun** or **light shade**. The potting mix should be **moist** and **well drained**. Water it regularly because this plant doesn't like to dry out completely. It does, however, recover quickly from wilting when watered. Fertilize every two weeks with quarter-strength fertilizer. Cuttings can be taken in late summer and grown indoors for use the following summer.

Tips

Fan flower is popular for hanging baskets and as an edging plant in a container where it can trail down. It is also an attractive filler plant in mixed containers, where the trailing habit will spread between other plants.

Recommended

S. aemula forms a mound of foliage from which trailing stems emerge. The fan-shaped flowers come in shades of purple, usually with white bases. **'Blue Wonder'** has long, trailing branches, making it ideal for hanging baskets. It can eventually spread 36" or more. **'Saphira'** is a compact variety with deep blue flowers. WHIRLWIND BLUE is a compact plant that bears heat- and fade-resistant, blue flowers. WHIRLWIND WHITE bears white flowers on compact, heat-tolerant plants.

S. aemula with canna lily, verbena and others

Features: bushy or trailing, decorative habit; blue, purple or white, fan-shaped flowers
Height: up to 8" **Spread:** up to 4'
Hardiness: tender perennial grown as an annual **Grow rating:** challenging

Flowering Maple
Abutilon

A. x *hybridum* (above & below)

Flowering maples suffered in reputation because their beautiful blooms were pendulous—they faced downward. Newer cultivars have addressed this condition, but as a class, flowering maples are handsome plants that can be treated as annuals, perennials or even small shrubs.

Growing

Flowering maple grows well in **full sun** or **light shade**. The potting mix should be **moist** and **well drained**. Fertilize every two weeks during the growing season with quarter- to half-strength fertilizer. This tender plant must be moved indoors in winter if it is to survive. Trim it back annually to keep the size manageable.

Tips

Flowering maple makes a stunning specimen, but it is also a lovely companion plant. Plant mounding and trailing annuals around the base of flowering maple to create a pretty display for your front entryway.

Recommended

*A. x **hybridum*** is a bushy shrub that grows 3–5' tall and bears downy, maple-like leaves on woody branches. The single flowers are pendulous and bell-shaped. There are a number of selections available in a variety of colors including peach, white, cream, yellow, orange, red or pink. **Bella Mix** from Ball Horticultural grows 14–16" tall with pastel flowers in yellow, ivory, pink, rose, coral, red, apricot or peach. **'Crimson Belle'** has deep red flowers.

Also called: Indian mallow, parlor maple
Features: pendulous flowers in shades of yellow, orange, red, pink or white; maple-like, sometimes variegated foliage **Height:** 14"–5'
Spread: 24–36" **Hardiness:** tender shrub grown as an annual or overwintered indoors
Grow rating: medium

Fuchsia
Fuchsia

Fuchsias are some of the most showy flowers for hanging baskets. Now there are cultivars with variegated foliage. Most fuchsias don't like heat and rarely revive if allowed to dry out.

Growing

Fuchsias grow best in **partial shade** or **light shade**. They are generally not tolerant of summer heat, so full sun can be too hot for them. The potting mix should be **moist** and **well drained**. Fertilize bi-weekly with half-strength fertilizer. Fuchsias should be dead-headed. Pluck the swollen seedpods from behind the fading petals. Plants can be overwintered indoors or thrown away at the end of the season.

Tips

Upright fuchsias can be used in mixed containers. Pendulous fuchsias are most often used in hanging baskets but also look great spilling over the edge of a large container.

Recommended

F. **Angels' Earrings Series** from Proven Winners are very heat- and humidity-tolerant plants that grow 10–12" tall.

F. x *hybrida* offers dozens of wonderful hybrids. The upright selections grow 18–36" tall, and the pendulous fuchsias grow 6–24" tall. **'Gartenmeister Bonstedt'** is an upright cultivar that grows about 24" tall and bears tubular, orange-red flowers. The foliage is bronzy red with purple undersides.

Fuchsias bloom on new growth, which will be stimulated by a high-nitrogen plant food.

F. x *hybrida* 'Gartenmeister Bonstedt'

Features: pink, orange, red, purple or white, often bicolored flowers; attractive foliage **Height:** 6–36" **Spread:** 6–36" **Hardiness:** tender shrub grown as an annual **Grow rating:** challenging

Geranium
Pelargonium

P. peltatum cultivar with lobelia

There are many more scented-leaf geraniums available. The foliage is not only fragrant, it is also often variegated and deeply lobed, sometimes even lacy-looking.

Features: decorative, often-colorful foliage; red, pink, violet, orange, salmon, white or purple, summer flowers **Height:** 8–24" **Spread:** 6"–4' **Hardiness:** tender perennial grown as an annual **Grow rating:** easy

Geraniums are perhaps the quintessential container plants. They match up well with many other plant shapes and are extremely tolerant of lackadaisical watering. Most are upright growers, but there are also trailing, ivy-leaved varieties. Try scented geraniums for their uniquely decorative and wonderfully fragrant foliage as well as for their flowers.

Growing
Geraniums prefer **full sun** but tolerate partial shade, although they may not bloom as profusely. The potting mix

should be **well drained**. Fertilize with quarter-strength fertilizer every one or two weeks during the growing season. Deadhead to keep geraniums blooming and looking neat, and pinch them back occasionally to keep plants bushy. Geraniums can be kept indoors over winter in a bright room.

Tips

With their brightly colored flowers and decorative foliage, geraniums are very popular for mixed containers, window boxes and hanging baskets.

Recommended

P. capitatum is a compact plant with irregularly shaped, rose-scented leaves. It bears pinkish purple flowers.

P. **'Chocolate Peppermint'** has green leaves with irregular, bronze-purple centers that smell like chocolaty peppermint. The flowers are pink and white.

P. crispum (lemon-scented geranium) forms a compact, low or upright mound of bright green, crinkly, lemon-scented foliage. It bears small, pink flowers in summer. **'Cream Peach'** has green, cream and yellow variegated, peach-scented foliage. **'Variegatum'** ('Variegated Prince Rupert') has ruffled, cream variegated, lemon-scented foliage.

P. x *hortorum* (zonal geranium) is a bushy plant with red, pink, purple, orange or white flowers and frequently banded or multi-colored foliage. The **Fireworks Collection** includes several cultivars with star-shaped flowers in several shades including red and pink. The maple leaf–shaped foliage is colorfully banded. Plants have a compact habit.

P. peltatum (ivy-leaved geranium) has thick, waxy leaves and a trailing habit. It bears loose clusters of colorful flowers. Many cultivars are available.

P. peltatum with portulaca in planter and petunias (above), *P. peltatum* cultivar with jasmine and bacopa (below)

Golden Hakone Grass
Hakonechloa

H. macra 'Aureola' with ligularia, begonia and lysimachia

Golden hakone grass forms an arching clump that spills over the sides of containers. It grows well in shade and has attractive, often pinkish fall color. It is a slow grower and a perennial, so it can be overwintered.

Growing
Golden hakone grass grows well in **light shade** or **partial shade**. The potting mix should be **moist** and **well drained**. Fertilize every two weeks during the growing season with quarter- to half-strength fertilizer. Plants may benefit from protection from temperature fluctuations in winter.

Tips
Golden hakone grass is one of the few grasses that grows well in shaded locations. Its texture and color are a good contrast to broad-leaved shade plants such as hosta and lungwort.

Recommended
H. macra forms a clump of bright green, arching, grass-like foliage that turns deep pink in fall, then bronze as winter sets in. Several cultivars are available. **'All Gold'** has pure gold leaves and is more upright and spiky in habit. **'Aureola'** has bright yellow foliage with narrow, green streaks. The foliage turns pink in fall.

This ornamental grass is native to Japan, where it grows on mountainsides and cliffs, often near streams and other water sources.

Also called: Japanese forest grass
Features: perennial grass; arching habit; fall color **Height:** 12–24" **Spread:** 12–24"
Hardiness: zones 5–8 **Grow rating:** medium

Golden Marguerite
Anthemis

Daisy-like flowers almost completely cover the fine, feathery foliage when these plants are in bloom. Deadheading is required to keep them blooming fully, but the aromatic foliage can make this chore palatable.

Growing
Golden marguerite grows best in **full sun**. The potting mix should be **well drained**. This plant is drought tolerant. Fertilize monthly with quarter-strength fertlizer. Most are perennials, but you can grow them as annuals.

Tips
Golden marguerite can be planted alone in specimen containers and is also a cheerful addition to mixed containers. The daisy-like flowers have a warm, welcoming appearance that makes them a good choice for containers placed near an entryway.

Recommended
A. tinctoria (golden marguerite) forms a mounded clump of foliage that is completely covered in bright or pale yellow, daisy-like flowers in summer. **'Charme'** (dwarf golden marguerite) is a compact plant that grows 12–16" tall and 12" wide with bright yellow flowers. **'Kelwayi'** produces an abundance of large, bright lemon yellow to golden yellow flowers and has gray-green foliage. **'Susan Mitchell'** grows 18–24" tall and bears yellow-centered, creamy white flowers. It has attractive, silvery green foliage.

A. tinctoria

Shear plants back as flowering finishes to encourage fresh growth and a second flush of flowers.

Also called: dyer's chamomile, marguerite daisy **Features:** mounding or spreading perennial; yellow, orange or cream, daisy-like, summer flowers; finely divided or feathery foliage **Height:** 8–36" **Spread:** 18–24" **Hardiness:** zones 3–8 **Grow rating:** medium

Hardy Geranium
Geranium

G. JOLLY BEE

Hardy geraniums are available in a wide range of heights and colors, but most gardeners seek those with blue and purple flowers. The simple flowers aren't exceptionally showy, but their constant presence is appreciated as other flowers come and go.

Growing

Hardy geraniums prefer to grow in **partial shade** or **light shade** but tolerate full sun. The potting mix should be **well drained**. Fertilize every two weeks during the growing season with quarter-strength fertilizer. Move containers to a sheltered location protected from temperature fluctuations in winter.

Also called: cranesbill **Features:** clump- or mound-forming perennial; white, red, pink, purple or blue, summer flowers; dense, often deeply divided foliage **Height:** 6–36" **Spread:** 12–36" **Hardiness:** zones 3–8 **Grow rating:** medium

Tips

These long-flowering plants have a sprawling growth habit that makes them great as fillers in mixed containers.

Recommended

G. 'Johnson's Blue' forms a spreading mat of foliage. Bright blue flowers are borne over a long period in summer.

G. JOLLY BEE is a vigorous, mounding plant with large, violet-blue flowers that bloom for an extended period in summer and orange to red fall color.

G. macrorrhizum (bigroot cranesbill) forms a spreading mound of fragrant foliage. This plant is quite drought tolerant. Flowers in variable shades of pink are borne in spring and early summer.

G. pratense (meadow cranesbill) forms an upright clump and bears clusters of white, blue or light purple flowers for a short period in early summer. It self-seeds freely. **'Summer Skies'** has double flowers in soft lavender blue.

G. sanguineum (bloody cranesbill, bloodred cranesbill) forms a dense, mounding clump and bears bright magenta flowers mostly in early summer and sporadically until fall. **'Album'** has white flowers and a more open habit than other cultivars. **'Elke'** is a low, wide plant bearing white-centered, hot pink flowers with thin, white edges. **'Elsbeth'** has light pink flowers with dark pink veins and bright red fall foliage. **'Max Frei'** bears bright carmine pink to magenta pink flowers. **'New Hampshire Purple'** produces large, dark rose-purple flowers. **'Shepherd's Warning'** grows 6" tall and has rosy pink flowers. **Var.** *striatum* is heat and drought tolerant. It has pale pink blooms with blood red veins.

G. 'Johnson's Blue' (above)
G. *pratense* 'Plenum Violaceum' (below)

Heliotrope
Heliotropium

H. arborescens ATLANTIS with angelonia, lobelia, sweet flag, licorice plant and sage

Scent is one of the most underrated qualities of a container. Heliotrope brings a strong, sweet fragrance into the garden, along with large clusters of deep purple flowers.

Growing
Heliotrope grows best in **full sun**. The potting mix should be **humus rich, moist** and **well drained**. Fertilize once a month during the growing season with quarter-strength fertilizer. Plants can be treated as houseplants in winter; keep them in a cool and sunny location indoors.

Tips
Combine purple-flowered heliotrope with yellow- or white-flowered plants and plants with burgundy foliage for striking color contrasts.

Recommended
H. arborescens is a low, bushy shrub that bears large clusters of sweet-scented, purple flowers all summer. Some new cultivars are not as strongly scented as the species. ATLANTIS, a Proven Selection by Proven Winners, is heat-tolerant and bears large, fragrant clusters of royal purple flowers. **'Basket Marino'** is a new, spreading plant that does well in hanging baskets. **'Black Beauty'** bears deep purple, fragrant flowers. **'Blue Wonder'** is a compact plant with heavily scented, dark purple flowers. **'Fragrant Delight'** has a vanilla fragrance in a compact plant.

Also called: cherry pie plant **Features:** bushy habit; purple or white, fragrant flowers; attractive foliage **Height:** 8–24" **Spread:** 12–24" **Hardiness:** tender shrub grown as an annual or overwintered indoors **Grow rating:** medium

These old-fashioned flowers may have been popular in your grandmother's garden. Their recent comeback is no surprise, considering their attractive foliage, flowers and scent.

Hens and Chicks

Sempervivum

Hens and chicks are easy to grow, multiply to fill spaces in containers and need little care other than a very well-drained soil and a light sprinkle of water during extended dry periods.

Growing

Hens and chicks grow well in **full sun** or **partial shade**. The potting mix should be **very well drained**. Add fine gravel or grit to the mix to provide adequate drainage. Fertilize once or twice during the growing season with quarter-strength fertilizer.

Tips

These plants can be used in shallow troughs and make interesting center-pieces on patio and picnic tables. They can also be combined with other drought-tolerant plants and succulents such as sedum in mixed containers.

Recommended

S. arachnoideum (cobweb houseleek) is identical to *S. tectorum* except that the tips of the leaves are entwined with hairy fibers, giving the appearance of cobwebs. This plant may need protection during wet weather.

S. tectorum is one of the most commonly grown hens and chicks of the many species, cultivars and hybrids available. It forms a low-growing mat of fleshy-leaved rosettes. Small, new rosettes are quickly produced and grow and multiply to fill almost any space. Flowers may be produced in summer. **'Atropurpureum'** has dark reddish purple leaves. **'Limelight'** has yellow-green, pink-tipped foliage. **'Pacific Hawk'** has dark red leaves that are edged with silvery hairs.

S. tectorum with phormium

These curious plants can grow on almost any surface. In the past, they were grown on tile roofs—it was believed they would protect the house from lightning.

Also called: houseleek **Features:** rosette-forming, succulent perennial; red, yellow, white or purple flowers **Height:** 2–6" **Spread:** 12" or more **Hardiness:** zones 3–8 **Grow rating:** easy

Hosta

Hosta

H. cultivar with others

Hosta leaves can be used in fresh flower arrangements.

Features: clump-forming perennial; decorative foliage in shades of green or variegated with yellow or cream; late summer or fall, mauve, purple or white flowers **Height:** 1–4' **Spread:** 18–36" **Hardiness:** zones 3–8 **Grow rating:** easy

There are almost endless variations in hosta foliage; swirls, stripes, puckers and ribs enhance the leaves' various sizes, shapes and colors. These popular shade perennials will need protection to get them through most Midwest winters.

Growing

Hostas prefer **light shade** or **partial shade** but will grow in full shade. Some will tolerate full sun. The potting mix should be **moist** and **well drained**. Fertilize plants monthly during the growing season with half-strength fertilizer. Move containers to a sheltered location in winter.

Tips

Hostas are wonderful woodland plants and look very attractive when combined with ferns and other fine-textured plants. Combine a variety of hostas together or mix them with other plants.

Recommended

Hostas have been subjected to a great deal of crossbreeding and hybridizing, resulting in hundreds of cultivars. The following are just a few of the possibilities. **'Baby Bunting'** is a popular cultivar with dark green to slightly bluish green, heart-shaped leaves and light purple flowers. **'Fragrant Bouquet'** has bright green leaves with creamy yellow margins and very fragrant, white flowers. **'Gold Standard'** is a hosta fancier's favorite, bearing bright yellow leaves with narrow, green margins. **'Guacamole'** has chartreuse leaves with dark green margins and fragrant, white flowers. **'June'** has bright yellow leaves with blue-green margins and light purple flowers. **'Pandora's Box'** forms a compact mound of creamy leaves with irregular green margins and bears light purple flowers. **'Tardiflora'** forms an attractive, small mound of dark green leaves and bears lots of light purple flowers in fall.

H. fortuneii 'Francee' (above), *H.* cultivar (center)

H. cultivar with coral bells and barberry (below)

Hydrangea
Hydrangea

H. paniculata LIMELIGHT

Try an Annabelle hydrangea with white-flowering daylilies and hostas and a silver-leaved lamium to create a beautiful, white garden in a shady corner.

Features: mounding, spreading or climbing, deciduous shrub or tree; clusters of white, pink, blue, purple or red flowers in summer; attractive foliage, sometimes with good fall color; some with exfoliating bark **Height:** 3–10' **Spread:** 3–10' **Hardiness:** zones 3–8 **Grow rating:** challenging

From rounded shrubs and small trees to climbing vines, hydrangeas offer a wealth of possibilities for use in containers.

Growing

Hydrangeas grow well in **full sun** or **partial shade**, but some species tolerate full shade. These plants perform best in cool conditions, and some shade will reduce leaf and flower scorch in hotter gardens. The potting mix should be

humus rich, moist and **well drained**. Fertilize monthly during the growing season with quarter- to half-strength fertilizer. Move containers to a sheltered location out of the wind and sun in winter.

Tips

Hydrangeas add a thriller element to mixed containers with their large flower clusters. Shrubby forms can be grown alone or combined with other plants. Tree forms are small enough to grow in containers but large enough to offer a good vertical accent. Climbing hydrangeas can be grown in a large container and used to create a beautiful display against a wall or over the edge of a balcony.

Recommended

H. anomala subsp. *petiolaris* (climbing hydrangea) is an elegant climbing plant with dark green, glossy leaves. It bears clusters of lacy-looking flowers in mid-summer. (Zones 4–8)

H. arborescens 'Annabelle' (Annabelle hydrangea) is a rounded shrub that bears large clusters of white flowers, even in shady conditions.

H. macrophylla (bigleaf hydrangea) is a rounded shrub that bears flowers in shades of pink, red, blue or purple from mid- to late summer. Many cultivars are available. (Zones 5–8)

H. paniculata 'Grandiflora' (Peegee hydrangea) is a spreading to upright large shrub or small tree that bears white flowers from late summer to early fall. (Zones 4–8)

H. quercifolia (oakleaf hydrangea) is a mound-forming shrub with attractive, cinnamon brown, exfoliating bark. Its large leaves are lobed like an oak's and turn bronze to bright red in fall. It bears conical clusters of sterile as well as fertile flowers. (Zones 4–8)

H. macrophylla (above & below)

Impatiens
Impatiens

I. walleriana at base of a Japanese maple

The name Impatiens *refers to the impatient nature of the seedpods. When ripe, the seedpods burst open with the slightest touch and scatter their seeds.*

Features: bushy or spreading habit; flowers in shades of purple, red, burgundy, pink, orange, salmon, apricot, yellow, white or bicolored **Height:** 6–36" **Spread:** 12–24" **Hardiness:** tender annual **Grow rating:** easy

Almost any combination shade planter can benefit from the addition of white or pastel impatiens.

Growing
Impatiens do best in **partial shade** or **light shade** but tolerate full shade or, if kept moist, full sun. New Guinea and balsam impatiens are best adapted to sunny locations. The potting mix should be **humus rich, moist** and **well drained**. Mix in some compost or earthworm

castings. Fertilize every two weeks with quarter-strength fertilizer.

Tips

These bushy or spreading plants make great colorful fillers in shady containers. Busy Lizzie is known for its ability to grow and flower profusely in deep shade. It looks lovely in hanging baskets and in planter boxes near a shady building entrance. New Guinea impatiens are almost shrubby in form and are grown as much for their variegated leaves as for their flowers. Balsam impatiens are more upright than either of the other two types and work great as the center plant in a container.

Recommended

I. balsamina (balsam impatiens) grows 12–36" tall and up to 18" wide. The flowers come in singles and doubles in shades of purple, red, pink or white.

I. hawkeri (New Guinea Group, New Guinea impatiens) are bushy plants with glossy, dark green foliage that is often variegated with a yellow stripe down the center. The flowers come in shades of red, orange, pink, purple or white. Plants grow 12–30" tall and 12" wide or wider.

I. walleriana with baby tears and vinca (above), *I. hawkeri* 'New Guinea' (below)

I. walleriana (busy Lizzie) is a bushy, spreading plant that grows 6–18" tall and up to 24" wide. The glossy leaves come in shades of light through dark green or bronze. The flowers come in shades of purple, red, burgundy, pink, orange, salmon, apricot, yellow, white or bicolored. **Fiesta Series** bears double flowers in shades of pink, orange, red and burgundy. Compact plants grow about 12" tall, with an equal spread. With their habit and flower form, they resemble small rose bushes. '**Victorian Rose**' is an All-America Selections winner with deep pink, double or semi-double flowers.

Iris

Iris

We normally think of tall bearded iris for this plant, but there are several other species that combine neat plant habit and shorter flower stalks to work well in combination planters. Japanese iris does well in a water container garden.

Growing

Irises grow best in **full sun** but tolerate partial shade or light shade. The potting mix should be **moist** and **well drained**, though several species are tolerant of dry conditions. Fertilize monthly during the growing season with quarter-strength fertilizer. Move containers to a sheltered location out of the wind and sun in winter.

Tips

Irises provide a wonderful strong, vertical accent. Several species grow in wet soil and can be combined with other moisture-lovers such as cardinal flower and elephant ears for a bog-themed container. There are iris flowers in almost every imaginable shade, and these can be used to create complementary or contrasting combinations in mixed containers.

Recommended

I. ensata (Japanese iris) is a water-loving species that bears blue, purple, pink or white flowers in early to mid-summer.

I. pallida (sweet iris, variegated iris) is a drought-tolerant, purple-flowered species that is rarely grown, but its variegated cultivars are a useful addition to mixed containers. 'Argentea Variegata' has cream-and-green-striped foliage. 'Aurea Variegata' has yellow-and-green-striped foliage.

Iris with others

Features: clump-forming, rhizomatous perennial; narrow or broad, strap-like, possibly variegated foliage; summer flowers in every shade of the rainbow **Height:** 1–4' **Spread:** 8–36" **Hardiness:** zones 2–8 **Grow rating:** medium

I. pseudacorus (yellow flag iris) is a moisture-loving species with narrow foliage and bright yellow, brown- or purple-marked flowers in mid- and late summer.

I. sibirica (Siberian iris) likes a moist but well-drained soil. It bears purple flowers in early summer, though cultivars with pink, blue, white, yellow or red flowers are available.

I. versicolor (blue flag iris) is a moisture-loving species that bears flowers in varied shades of purple in early summer.

Irises are steeped in history and lore. The name Iris *comes from the Greek messenger to the gods, who travelled using the rainbow as a bridge.*

I. pseudacorus (below)

Japanese Painted Fern
Athyrium

A. niponicum var. *pictum* 'Silver Falls'

The demand for these wonderful ferns will certainly encourage enthusiastic breeders to create more varieties.

Features: deciduous, perennial fern; decorative foliage **Height:** 1–4' **Spread:** 1–4' **Hardiness:** zones 4–8 **Grow rating:** easy

Delicate, decorative and well behaved, *Athyrium* is one of the few fern genera really suitable for container culture. They are perennial, but be aware that some of the newer Japanese painted fern culitvars are slow to re-emerge after winter.

Growing

This fern grows well in **full shade, partial shade** or **light shade**. The potting mix should be **acidic** and **moist**. Fertilize every two weeks during the growing season with quarter-strength fertilizer. It will need some protection in winter. Cover it if it will be left outdoors, or move it to a sheltered location.

Tips

Create a woodland understory in a pot. Combine hosta, coral bells, Annabelle hydrangea and either *Athyrium* species in a large planter for a shaded location. These ferns make an attractive addition to almost any mixed planter combination and will perform admirably as long as they don't get too much sun.

Recommended

A. felix-femina (lady fern) forms a dense clump of lacy fronds. The appearance can be quite variable because the leaflets on the fronds and the fronds themselves are prone to dividing, giving the plants a more lacy appearance or sometimes even a dense, ball-like appearance. It varies in size from dwarfs that grow 12" tall and wide to larger plants that can grow 2–4' tall and wide. Interesting cultivars include **'Dre's Dagger,'** with narrow leaflets arranged in four rows around each frond, and **'Encourage,'** whose leaflets are divided at the tips, giving a frilly or fan-like appearance to the outer edges of each frond. Somewhat harder to find, but interesting nonetheless, is **'Acrocladon,'** whose fronds subdivide so often that the fern appears to be a small, dense ball of foliage.

A. niponicum var. *pictum* (Japanese painted fern) is a low, creeping fern with reddish to burgundy stems and a silvery metallic sheen to the bronzy fronds. Several cultivars have been developed with varied frond colors. **'Burgundy Lace'** has pinkish purple fronds with a metallic sheen. **'Silver Falls'** has silvery metallic fronds with striking, reddish purple stems and veins.

A. niponicum var. *pictum* with iris, heucherella and others (above), *A. felix-femina* (below)

Lady's Mantle
Alchemilla

A. mollis

The chartreuse flower sprays make interesting substitutes for baby's breath in fresh and dried arrangements.

Few perennials look as captivating as lady's mantle does with droplets of morning dew clinging like shimmering pearls to its velvety leaves.

Growing

Lady's mantle grows well in **light shade** or **partial shade** with protection from the afternoon sun. Hot locations and excessive sun will scorch the leaves. The potting mix should be **humus rich, moist** and **well drained**. Fertilize every two weeks during the growing season with quarter-strength fertilizer. Leaves can be sheared back in summer if they begin to look tired and heat stressed; new leaves will emerge. Move containers to a sheltered location where they will be protected from temperature fluctuations in winter.

Tips

Lady's mantle is an ideal filler for mixed containers, where it has a visually softening effect. Combine it with yellow- and purple-flowered annuals for an elegant, contrasting combination.

Recommended

A. alpina (alpine lady's mantle) is a low-growing plant that reaches 3–5" in height and spreads about 20". Clusters of tiny, yellow flowers are borne in summer.

A. mollis (common lady's mantle) forms a mound of soft, rounded foliage and produces sprays of frothy-looking, yellowish green flowers in early summer. It grows 8–18" tall and spreads about 24".

Features: mound-forming perennial; yellow or yellow-green, summer and early-fall flowers; attractive, downy foliage **Height:** 2–18" **Spread:** 18–24" **Hardiness:** zones 3–8 **Grow rating:** medium

Lamium

Lamium

L. maculatum 'White Nancy,' a Proven Winners Selection, with others

These plants, with their striped, dotted or banded, silver and green foliage, provide a summer-long attraction and thrive on the barest neccessities of life. Lamiums may self-seed into garden beds, where they can become invasive.

The striking foliage is great for brightening up dark nooks and corners. The plants look especially lovely at dusk and in the moonlight.

Growing

Lamium grows well in **light shade** or **partial shade** with protection from the

Features: spreading or trailing perennial; decorative, variegated foliage; pink, white, yellow or purple, small, summer flowers **Height:** 6–12" **Spread:** 12–24" **Hardiness:** zones 2–8 **Grow rating:** easy

L. maculatum 'Beacon Silver' with impatiens (above)
L. galeobdolon 'Florentium' with others (below)

hot afternoon sun. The potting mix should be **moist** and **well drained**. Fertilize no more than once a month during the growing season with quarter-strength fertilizer. Lamium is one of the easier perennials to bring through winter. Move the container to a sheltered location in winter where the plant will be protected from temperature fluctuations.

Tips

Lamium is a stunning foliage plant, and its spreading nature makes it a fantastic filler plant in mixed containers. It will trail over the edges of containers and hanging baskets.

Recommended

L. galeobdolon (*Lamiastrum galeobdolon*; yellow archangel, false lamium) is a mounding, spreading plant with silver-marked leaves and short spikes of yellow flowers in summer. **'Florentium'** ('Variegatum') is a low-growing cultivar with silvery leaves edged in green. **'Hermann's Pride'** forms a dense mat of white-speckled leaves. **'Silver Angel'** is a spreading plant with silvery foliage. (Zones 3–8)

L. maculatum (spotted dead nettle) is a low-growing, spreading plant with green leaves with white or silvery markings. It bears short spikes of pink, white or mauve flowers in summer. **'Anne Greenaway'** has silver, green and yellow variegated leaves and lavender flowers. **'Aureum'** has variegated chartreuse and silver foliage and pink flowers. **'Beacon Silver'** has silvery leaves with dark green margins and pink flowers. **'Orchid Frost'** has silvery foliage edged in blue-green and bears deep pink blooms. **'White Nancy,'** a Proven Selection by Proven Winners, has silvery white foliage and white flowers.

Lantana

Lantana

*L*antana is a can't-miss container plant because of its range and combination of colors, its informal, sprawling habit, its ability to attract butterflies and its low-maintenance requirements.

Growing
Lantana grows best in **full sun** but tolerates partial shade. The potting mix should be **fertile, moist** and **well drained**, but lantana can handle heat and drought. Feed every two weeks with quarter-strength fertilizer.

Tips
Lantana adds color and volume to mixed containers and works great as a specimen. It also looks great in hanging baskets.

Recommended
L. camara is a bushy plant that bears round clusters of flowers in many colors. **Lucky Series** plants grow 10–14" tall, have a neat, upright habit and do well in the heat and with restricted water. **'New Gold'** grows 24" tall and bears clusters of bright yellow flowers.

L. **Patriot Series** come in a wide range of colors. Their dark to mid-green foliage has a minty fragrance. **'Dove Wings'** gracefully grows 24" tall and 12" wide and produces pure white flowers. **'Rainbow'** is a compact plant that grows 12" tall and wide. It has large, dark green foliage and yellow, orange or pink flowers.

L. montevidensis **'Weeping Lavender'** is a weeping or sprawling plant with slender stems that trail to 36". It produces dense clusters of pinkish lilac flowers.

L. camara LUSCIOUS SERIES 'Tropicial Fruit' from Proven Winners

Take cuttings in late summer to start plants for the following summer if you don't want to store a large plant over winter.

Also called: shrub verbena **Features:** yellow, orange, pink, purple, red or white flowers, often in combination; attractive foliage **Height:** 12–36" **Spread:** 12–36" **Hardiness:** tender shrub grown as an annual **Grow rating:** easy

Lavender
Lavandula

L. angustifolia

Midwest winters can be harsh on lavenders, but we continue to use these scented, purple-blooming marvels in herb gardens nonetheless.

Growing
Lavender grows best in **full sun**. The potting mix should be **alkaline** and **well drained**. Established plants tolerate heat and drought. Fertilize monthly during the growing season with quarter-strength fertilizer. In winter, move containers to a sheltered location and cover them, or move them to an unheated shed or garage.

Tips
Lavender is a wonderful, aromatic plant that makes a good shrubby addition to mixed containers. Good companions include other drought-tolerant specimens, such as thyme and sedum.

Recommended
L. angustifolia (English lavender) bears spikes of small flowers in varied shades of purple from mid-summer to fall. **'Hidcote'** bears deep purple flowers. **'Jean Davis'** is a compact cultivar with pale pink flowers. **'Lady'** bears purple flowers and grows from seed to flower the first summer. **'Munstead'** is the hardiest lavender for the Midwest. **'Thumbelina'** grows 6–12" tall and wide with violet-blue blooms.

L. x intermedia is a rounded shrub with blue or purple flowers held on long stems. **'Provence'** is a rot resistant cultivar that grows 24–36" tall.

L. stoechas (French lavender) is a compact, bushy plant bearing dark purple flowers. **'Kew Red'** bears bright pink flowers with light pink bracts. (Zone 8)

Features: bushy, woody shrub; narrow, gray-green leaves; spikes of purple, pink or blue, mid-summer to fall flowers **Height:** 6–36"
Spread: 6–24" **Hardiness:** zones 5–8
Grow rating: medium

Lemon
Citus

Part of the fun of container gardening is growing something unique. 'Meyer' lemon is relatively small and has fragrant white blooms in late winter and harvestable fruit. Note that these trees need four hours of sunlight even throughout the winter while indoors.

Growing

Lemons grow best in a sheltered location in **full sun** but will tolerate partial shade as long as they get four hours of direct sunlight daily. The planting mix should be **well drained** and **slightly acidic**. Allow the top of the soil to dry out slightly between waterings. Feed with half-strength fertilizer every two weeks during the growing season, but taper off as winter approaches.

When temperatures approach 45° F, move to a sunny location indoors. You can use artificial grow lights. Don't worry if the plant drops its leaves; they will grow back. Reduce watering in winter, but do not allow the soil to dry out completely. Move the tree outdoors when temperatures stay above 50° F at night. Harden off the plant before placing it in full sun.

Repot when the tree becomes rootbound, about every 2–3 years. Prune in spring to control the size or improve the shape.

Tips

You can pollinate the flowers that bloom indoors if fruit is desired. Take a small, soft brush and dust pollen from one flower to another.

Recommended

C. limon '**Meyer**' (*C. meyeri*) and '**Meyer Improved**' (virus-free) are dwarf trees with sparsely thorned branches

and shiny, dark green foliage. They can grow 12' tall and 10' wide but are usually much smaller when grown in a container. The rounded, yellow, sometimes orange-tinged, thin-skinned fruits may take a year to develop. Plants are self-pollinating, so a second variety is not required.

Features: fragrant flowers; edible fruit; attractive foliage **Height:** 3–6' in containers **Spread:** 3–5' in containers **Hardiness:** zones 9–10; overwinter indoors **Grow rating:** challenging

Licorice Plant
Helichrysum

H. petiolare 'Petite Licorice' with dusty miller

Licorice plant is a good indicator for hanging baskets—when you see the plant wilting, it is time to get out the hose or watering can.

Conjure up the chewy candy, and it's a stretch to imagine the connection to this silvery, satiny foliage plant. Licorice plant's silvery sheen is caused by a fine, soft pubescence on its leaves.

Growing

Licorice plant prefers **full sun**. The potting mix should be **neutral to alkaline** and **well drained**. Licorice plant wilts if the soil dries out but revives quickly once watered. It is easy to start more plants from cuttings in fall, giving you a supply of new plants for the following spring. Once they have rooted, keep the young plants in a cool, bright room during winter.

Tips

Licorice plant provides horizontal growth to fill in a container or spill over the side. Its lack of flowers makes it a complementary element to colorful flowering plants.

Recommended

H. petiolare is a trailing plant with fuzzy, gray-green leaves. The cultivars are more common than the species. **'Lemon Licorice'** has yellow-green foliage. **'Licorice Splash'** and **'Variegata'** have gray-green leaves with irregular, creamy margins. **'Limelight'** has bright lime green leaves. **'Petite Licorice'** is a compact selection with small, gray-green leaves. **'Silver'** has gray-green leaves covered in a silvery white down. **'White Licorice'** has silvery white foliage. **'Minus'** is a compact plant with small, silver leaves, and it can be grown easily from seed.

H. thianschanicum **'Icicles'** is a compact plant that has long, needle-like, silver foliage.

Features: bushy or trailing habit; downy, gray-green, silvery, yellow or cream and green variegated foliage **Height:** 6–24" **Spread:** 1–4' **Hardiness:** tender perennial or shrub grown as an annual **Grow rating:** easy

Lobelia
Lobelia

L. *erinus* cultivars and others (above),
L. *erinus* (below)

Annual lobelia is commonly used in containers for its mounding habit and blue colors, but perennial lobelia (cardinal flower) can also be worked into combination planters. In warmer areas, look for the annual Laguna Series, which has superior heat resistance.

Growing

Lobelia grows well in **full sun** or **partial shade**, with partial or light shade preferable for annual lobelia in hot and humid areas. The potting mix should be **humus rich, moist** and **well drained**. Cardinal flower tolerates wet soil. Fertilize every two to four weeks during the growing season with quarter-strength fertilizer.

Features: bushy to upright habit; purple, blue, pink, white or red, summer to fall flowers
Height: 4–24" **Spread:** 6" or more
Hardiness: zones 4–8; annual **Grow rating:** medium

L. erinus 'Sapphire' with lamium and impatiens (above)
L. cardinalis (below)

Cardinal flower should be moved to a sheltered location, preferably an unheated garage, in winter.

Tips

Use annual lobelia in mixed containers or hanging baskets. The delicate, airy appearance adds a glaze of color that looks particularly attractive with broad-leaved plants such as hosta and lady's mantle.

Cardinal flower has a more upright habit, and its often bronzy foliage gives mixed containers an elegant appearance. Its ability to grow in moist to wet soil makes it suitable for boggy containers with other moisture lovers.

Recommended

L. cardinalis (cardinal flower) is a perennial that forms an upright clump of bronzy green foliage. It bears spikes of bright red flowers in summer and fall.

L. erinus (annual lobelia) may be rounded and bushy or low and trailing. It bears flowers in shades of blue, purple, red, pink or white. **Laguna Series** has heat-resisitant, trailing plants with flowers in a variety of colors. **Riviera Series** has flowers in shades of blue and purple on compact, bushy plants.

L. x speciosa (hybrid cardinal flower) is a vigorous, bushy perennial. Hardiness varies from hybrid to hybrid. It bears flowers in shades of red, blue, purple, pink or white in summer and fall.

Trim annual lobelia back after the first wave of flowers. It will stop blooming in the hottest part of summer but usually revives in fall.

Lotus Vine

Lotus

*L*otus vine is a fine spiller element for planter boxes and decorative containers with its arching stems of fine, grayish green foliage. If grown well, it will produce blooms that resemble a parrot's beak.

Growing

Lotus vine grows well in **full sun** or **partial shade**. The potting mix should be **well drained**. This annual can tolerate hot and dry locations. Pinch the new tips back in late spring or early summer to promote bushier growth. Fertilize monthly with quarter-strength fertilizer.

Tips

Lotus vine is most effective when its striking, unique foliage is allowed to cascade over the side of a decorative pot, window box or planter. The flowers are bright and colorful, and they contrast with the silvery green, ferny foliage. Lotus vine complements purple- and yellow-flowering annuals and chartreuse- or bronze-leaved foliage plants very nicely.

Recommended

L. berthelotii is a trailing plant with silvery stems covered in fine, soft, needle-like foliage. Small clusters of vivid orange to scarlet flowers that resemble lobster claws are borne in spring and summer.

L. hirsutus is a bushy or trailing perennial with fine, gray-green foliage. It bears pink-flushed, white flowers in summer and fall.

L. x 'Amazon Sunset' has gray-green, needle-like foliage and vibrantly hued yellow-orange, beak-like flowers in April and May.

L. berthelotii with pansies

Lotus vine is also known as parrot's beak, coral gem and pelican's beak, names that make reference to the flowers' appearance.

Features: bushy or trailing habit; orange, red or yellow, summer through fall flowers **Height:** 6–8" **Spread:** 36" or more **Hardiness:** tender perennial grown as an annual **Grow rating:** easy

Maidenhair Fern
Adiantum

A. pedatum with dracaena, oxalis and coleus

These fine-textured plants give mixed containers a light, airy appearance.

Features: deciduous fern; summer and fall foliage; habit **Height:** 12–36" **Spread:** 12–24" **Hardiness:** zones 3–8; tender perennial grown as an annual **Grow rating:** easy

These delicate-looking ferns add a graceful touch to any shady container planting. Their unique habit and texture will stand out in any combination.

Growing
Maidenhair fern grows well in **partial shade** or **light shade** but tolerates full shade. The potting mix should be **humus rich, slightly acidic** and **moist.** Fertilize monthly during the growing season with quarter-strength fertilizer. Move northern maidenhair fern to a sheltered location in winter. Bring giant maidenhair fern indoors and keep it in a cool, bright room in winter.

Tips
These ferns will do well in any shaded spot. Include them in mixed containers, where they make beautiful, arching companions to other shade-lovers such as hosta, lungwort and coral bells. They also look nice with colorful flowers.

Recommended
A. formosum (giant maidenhair fern) is a tender species that is sometimes grown as a houseplant. It has stunning, arching fronds that give the whole plant a cascading appearance. It is worth searching for and including in a mixed container, where it is sure to be an elegant beauty.

A. pedatum (northern maidenhair fern) is a hardy perennial that forms a spreading mound of delicate, arching fronds arranged in a horseshoe or circular pattern. Its light green leaflets stand out against the black stems and turn bright yellow in fall.

Mandevilla

Mandevilla

*L*arge, trumpet-shaped blooms on sun-loving vines set a tropical tone.

Growing

Mandevillas grow best in **full sun** with some protection from the hottest after-noon sun, but also do well in partial shade. The planting mix should be **well drained** and **moist**, with lots of compost mixed in. Allow the planting mix to dry slightly between waterings. Feed twice a month during the growing season with quarter- to half-strength fertilizer. Pinch young plants to induce bushiness.

Move plants indoors before the first frost into a bright location above 45° F. Cut back on watering but do not allow the soil to completely dry out. Pinch back weak growth throughout winter. Move plants outdoors when the risk of frost has passed. Prune out old or crowded stems before new growth begins.

Tips

Mandevillas can be trained to climb almost any sturdy structure. They look wonderful as specimens in trellised containers and hanging baskets.

Recommended

M. x *amabilis* has oval leaves and comes in a range of colors. **'Alice du Pont'** bears clusters of trumpet-shaped, pink, 2–4" flowers from spring through fall.

M. boliviensis has elliptic to oblong leaves and white, 2–4" flowers that bloom all summer.

M. SUN PARASOL SERIES are bushy, fast-growing vines that bear pink, white or red, 4–6" flowers all season long. MINI SUN PARASOL SERIES bear smaller flowers, up to 2" across, and elliptic foliage is often tinted red.

M. splendens has oval leaves and bears clusters of trumpet-shaped, pale pink, 2–4" flowers from spring through fall. The flowers fade to rosy pink with age. **'Red Riding Hood'** has bright to deep red flowers.

Features: woody-based, evergreen, twining vine; pink, red or white; showy flowers; glossy, dark green, foliage **Height:** often 3–6' for annuals, but can reach 12' **Spread:** 2–4' **Hardiness:** tender perennial grown as an annual **Grow rating:** easy

Maple
Acer

A. ginnala 'Bailey Compact'

Maple fruits, called samaras, have wings that act like miniature helicopter rotors and help in seed dispersal.

Features: small, multi-stemmed, deciduous tree or large shrub; colorful or decorative foliage that turns stunning shades of red, yellow or orange in fall **Height:** 2–15' **Spread:** 2–15' **Hardiness:** zones 2–8 **Grow rating:** medium

Trees are often considered too large for crowded residential areas, but several maples can be pruned and trained to fit your patio or balcony. Make sure to plant your maple in a large enough container. As the tree grows, be sure to anchor it against wind damage.

Growing

Maples do well in **full sun** or **light shade**. The potting mix should be **humus rich** and **well drained**. Fertilize no more than monthly during the growing season with quarter-strength fertilizer. Tender maples should be moved into a shed or garage in winter. Hardy maples will do fine in a spot protected from temperature fluctuations.

Tips

Maples can be used as specimen trees in containers on patios. A Japanese-style garden can be created in containers with a maple or two to add height and volume. Almost all maples can be used to create bonsai specimens.

Recommended

A. ginnala (amur maple) is an extremely hardy, rounded to spreading multi-stemmed shrub or small tree that has attractive, dark green leaves, bright red samaras and smooth bark with distinctive vertical striping. The fall foliage is often a brilliant crimson. The color develops best in full sun, but the tree will also grow well in light shade.

A. griseum (paperbark maple) is a slow-growing, rounded to oval tree with exfoliating, orange-brown bark that peels and curls away from the trunk in papery strips. The foliage turns red, orange or yellow in fall. (Zones 4–8)

A. japonicum (fullmoon maple, Japanese maple) is an open, spreading tree or large shrub. The leaves turn stunning shades of yellow, orange or red in fall. (Zones 5–7)

A. palmatum (Japanese maple) is a rounded, spreading or cascading, small tree that develops red, yellow or orange fall color. Types without dissected leaves, derived from ***A. p.* var. *atropurpureum***, are grown for their purple foliage. Types with dissected leaves, derived from ***A. p.* var. *dissectum***, have foliage so deeply lobed and divided that it appears fern-like or even thread-like. The leaves can be green, red or purple. (Zones 6–8)

A. palmatum 'Bloodgood' (above)

A. japonicum (center), *A. griseum* (below)

Maracas Brazilian Fireworks
Porphyrocoma

Maracas Brazilian fireworks can be moved indoors and placed in a bright window during winter. It can also be grown strictly as a houseplant.

Maracas Brazilian fireworks is a fairly new annual that brings hot, uniquely shaped flowers to the darkest shade gardens. True to its tropical nature, it endures hot summers and will bloom all season with reasonable care and some deadheading.

Growing
Maracas Brazilian fireworks grows well in **partial shade, light shade** or **full shade**. Early morning sun is acceptable, but keep these plants out of afternoon sun. The potting mix should be **humus rich, moist** and **well drained**. It is okay to let the potting mix dry out slightly between waterings. This plant self-seeds and can spread quickly, so make sure to deadhead. Plants may suffer if exposed to temperatures below 45° F for an extended period.

Tips
Maracas Brazilian fireworks is a great plant to use as a specimen or to mix with other shade-tolerant plants, such as coleus, to add bright color in the darker parts of your garden.

Recommended
P. pohliana is a Simply Beautiful® selection from Ball Horticultural Company and PanAmerican Seeds. It is a mounded to upright plant with purple flowers that emerge from red or pink bracts. The evergreen leaves are dark green with prominent silver veins.

Also called: rose pine cone **Features:** attractive variegated foliage; colorful flowers that bloom all summer **Height:** 6–12"
Spread: 8–18" **Hardiness:** zones 10–11; tender perennial grown as an annual
Grow rating: easy

Million Bells

Calibrachoa

C. Superbells Series 'Trailing Blue'

When well grown, these plants are covered with miniature, petunia-like blooms. Million bells are one of the best flowers to attract hummingbirds.

Growing

Million bells prefer to grow in **full sun**. The potting mix should be **moist** and **well drained**. Fertilize every two weeks with half-strength fertilizer. Although they prefer to be watered regularly, million bells are fairly drought resistant in cool and warm climates. They will bloom well into fall.

Tips

Million bells are excellent for hanging baskets, typically by themselves. They are also great as spillers for combination containers and window boxes.

Recommended

C. **hybrids** have a dense, trailing habit. They all bear small, yellow-centered flowers. Many series are available, including **Million Bells**, the first on the market; **Superbells**, which has larger flowers and semi-upright plants that are more heat resistant; **Colorburst**, with an arching, cascading habit; and **Starlette**, an upright series with non-stop blooming. Most series are available with flowers in shades of blue, purple, pink, red, yellow, orange or white. Several bicolored options are also available.

Also called: calibrachoa **Features:** trailing habit; pink, purple, blue, red, yellow, orange, white or bicolored flowers **Height:** 6–12" **Spread:** 24" **Hardiness:** tender perennial grown as an annual **Grow rating:** medium

Mondo Grass
Ophiopogon

O. planiscapus NIGRA

Mondo grass is often used as a border plant along flowerbeds and at the base of trees in the South. It is similar in appearance and growth to Liriope.

Features: low, clump-forming grass; uniquely colored foliage; lavender, pink or white flowers
Height: 4–12" **Spread:** 6–12"
Hardiness: zones 5–9; grown as an annual
Grow rating: easy

Mondo grass is a low-growing plant whose narrow leaf blades arch outward from a mounded habit, giving it a dome quality. The flowers are light purple. This plant is not a grass, but a member of the lily family.

Growing

Mondo grass grows best in **full sun** or **light shade**. The potting mix should be **humus rich, moist** and **well drained**. Fertilize monthly during the growing season with quarter- to half-strength fertilizer. Treat these plants like annuals or move containers to an unheated garage or shed in winter to protect them from temperature fluctuations.

Tips

Mondo grass is a good filler for combination containers. Its foliage contrasts nicely with colorful plants and looks attractive enough on its own when its companions are done blooming.

Recommended

O. japonicus (mondo grass, monkey grass) produces an evergreen mat of lush, dark green, grass-like foliage. Short spikes of white, occasionally lilac-tinged flowers emerge in summer, followed by metallic blue fruit. Many cultivars are available. Plants are hardy to zone 6 with protection.

O. planiscapus 'Ebknizam' (EBONY NIGHT) has curving, almost black leaves and dark lavender flowers. NIGRA (black mondo grass, black lily turf), a Proven Selection by Proven Winners, is a clumping, spreading plant with dark purple, almost black leaves and pink to mauve flowers.

Nasturtium
Tropaeolum

T. majus 'Jewel'

Nasturtiums' red, orange or yellow blooms and speckled foliage make a powerful statement in a terra-cotta pot.

Growing

Nasturtiums prefer **full sun** but tolerate some shade. The potting mix should be **light, moist** and **well drained**. Too much fertilizer will result in lots of leaves and very few flowers, so fertilize no more than monthly with quarter-strength fertilizer. Let the soil drain completely between waterings.

Tips

The climbing varieties can be grown up trellises or left to spill over the edge of a container and ramble around. The bushy selections can be used in mixed containers with other red-, yellow- or orange-flowered plants, or with other edible-flowered plants such as pansies for a themed container.

Recommended

T. majus is a bushy, trailing or climbing plant. It bears bright red, yellow or orange flowers all summer. The bright green leaves are round with wavy margins. **'Alaska'** has cream-mottled foliage and a bushy habit. **'Jewel'** has bushy plants with flowers in shades of red, scarlet, pink, yellow, cream or orange, some with darker-veined throats.

Features: trailing, climbing or bushy habit; bright red, orange, yellow, scarlet, pink, cream, gold, white or bicolored flowers; attractive, round, sometimes variegated foliage; edible leaves and flowers **Height:** 12–18" for dwarf varieties; up to 10' for trailing varieties **Spread:** equal to height **Hardiness:** annual **Grow rating:** medium

Nemesia
Nemesia

N. SUNSATIA PINEAPPLE with others

Profusions of tiny blooms make nemesias a fine choice to combine with larger flowering or textural plants in sunny combination containers.

Growing

Nemesias grow best in **full sun**. The potting mix should be **slightly acidic, moist** and **well drained**. Regular watering will keep these plants blooming through summer. Fertilize every two weeks with quarter-strength fertilizer when plants are actively growing and blooming. Nemesias benefit from being cut back hard when the flowering cycle slows.

Features: bushy, mound-forming or trailing habit; red, blue, purple, pink, white, yellow, orange or bicolored flowers **Height:** 6–24"
Spread: 4–12" **Hardiness:** annual; tender perennial grown as an annual
Grow rating: medium

Tips

Nemesia is an good choice as a combination spiller/filler for hanging baskets and window boxes.

Recommended

N. **hybrids** are bushy and mound-forming or trailing and have bright green foliage. They bear flowers in shades of blue, purple, white, pink, red or yellow, often in bicolors. **'Bluebird'** bears lavender blue flowers on low, bushy plants. **Carnival Series** plants are compact and bear many flowers in yellow, white, orange, pink or red. **'KLM'** has bicolored blue and white flowers with yellow throats. Proven Winners Selections SUNSATIA SERIES plants include colorful cultivars that may be bushy or trailing and several that are heat resistant.

Nicotiana
Nicotiana

These bushy, sticky plants topped with clusters of tubular flowers attract night-flying pollinators such as moths. Place them where you can enjoy their evening fragrance.

Growing
Nicotiana will grow equally well in **full sun, light shade** or **partial shade**. The potting mix should be **humus rich, moist** and **well drained**. Fertilize every two weeks with half-strength fertilizer.

Tips
The dwarf selections seem best suited for small mixed containers and can be used as fillers, but the taller selections make excellent thrillers with low, bushy and trailing plants surrounding their feet.

Recommended
N. alata is upright and has a strong, sweet fragrance. **Merlin Series** has dwarf plants with red, pink, purple, white or pale green flowers. **Nicki Series** has compact or dwarf plants with fragrant blooms in many colors.

N. **'Lime Green'** is an upright plant that bears clusters of lime green flowers.

N. sylvestris is a tall, upright plant that bears white blooms that are fragrant in the evening.

Nicotiana was originally cultivated for the wonderfully scented, green flowers that opened only in the evening and at night. In attempts to expand the variety of colors and have the flowers open during the day, the popular scent has, in some cases, been lost.

N. alata Nicki Series and *N. sylvestris* with spider flower

Features: rosette-forming to bushy, upright habit; red, pink, green, yellow, white or purple, sometimes fragrant flowers **Height:** 1–5' **Spread:** 12" **Hardiness:** annual **Grow rating:** medium

Oregano
Origanum

O. vulgare var. *hirtum* 'Aureum' with marigold, parsley and tarragon

Oregano, like basil, comes in many types, which is a perfect excuse to plant several in the same container and sample the different smells and flavors throughout summer.

Growing

Oregano grows best in **full sun**. The potting mix should be **neutral to alkaline** and **well drained**. Fertilize no more than once a month during the growing season with quarter-strength fertilizer. In winter, move hardy plants to a sheltered location; where they are not hardy, move them to an unheated shed or garage.

Tips

Try growing several different oreganos in individual containers of different heights to create a grouping, or plant different herbs in each pot for a more varied display.

Recommended

O. laevigatum is a shrubby, upright perennial that bears rosy purple flowers. **'Hopley's Purple'** bears dark purple flowers and is hardy to zone 6.

O. vulgare **var.** *hirtum* (oregano, Greek oregano) is a low-growing, bushy plant with hairy, gray-green leaves and white flowers. **'Aureum'** has bright golden leaves and pink flowers. **'Aureum Crispum'** has a spreading habit and curly, golden leaves. **'Zorba Red'** has a spreading habit with bright red-purple bracts and white flowers. **'Zorba White'** has greenish bracts and white flowers.

In Greek, oros means "mountain" and ganos means "joy" or "beauty," so oregano translates as "joy or beauty of the mountain."

Features: bushy perennial; fragrant, sometimes colorful foliage; white or pink, summer flowers **Height:** 10–24" **Spread:** 8–12" **Hardiness:** zones 5–9 **Grow rating:** easy

Ornamental Pepper
Capsicum

Ornamental peppers are grown for their miniature fruits that turn an array of colors as they mature. While they are edible, most are fiery hot, and gloves are recommended if you decide to cut them open to collect seeds.

Growing
Ornamental peppers like **full sun**. The planting mix should be **fertile, moist**, and **well drained**, with organic amendments such as compost. Don't let the soil dry out; the plants will wilt, and the result will be stunted growth and little or no fruit. Fertilize every two weeks with half-strength fertilizer. Wait until the risk of frost has passed and the soil has warmed before setting out transplants in your containers.

Tips
Ornamental peppers are the perfect edible addition to any sunny setting. Choose companions with flower and foliage colors complementary to the fruit color. Ornamental peppers are great as specimens in decorative containers. For maximum impact, plant peppers in groups because single specimens tend to get lost amid other plants.

Recommended
C. annuum closely resembles plants grown strictly for fruit but is often slightly smaller. Inconspicuous, white or yellow, summer flowers are followed by shiny, conical fruit. The fruits emerge pale cream and yellow but slowly mature into shades of purple, orange, yellow or red. The many cultivars offer variegated foliage and spherical fruit in varied colors. **'Explosive Ember'** is a new cultivar bearing dark purple foliage and fruit that matures to a bright red.

C. annuum cultivar

The colorful fruit can be dried and used in crafts and arrangements.

Features: colorful, shiny, waxy, edible (possibly hot) fruit; attractive habit **Height:** 6–36"
Spread: 6–24" **Hardiness:** tender annual
Grow rating: easy

Oxalis
Oxalis

O. vulcanicola 'Zinfandel' with others

Small pots of O. crassipes *are often found in garden centers and gift shops around St. Patrick's Day.*

Features: bushy or spreading habit; colorful foliage; yellow, white or pink flowers
Height: 6–12" **Spread:** 6–12" or more
Hardiness: tender perennial grown as an annual **Grow rating:** easy

Often called shamrock plant, this delicate filler is actually a perennial. Some varieties are hardy to zone 5. Small flowers emerge between the canopy of shamrocks, often in compelling, complementary colors.

Growing

Oxalis prefers **full sun** or **partial shade** but tolerates full shade with reduced flowering. The potting mix should be **humus rich** and **well drained**. Fertilize every two weeks with quarter-strength fertilizer.

Tips

Oxalis is becoming increasingly popular for container culture. It works well mixed with other plants and is equally stunning all by itself.

Recommended

O. crassipes is a vigorous, mound-forming species with bright green leaves and lemon yellow flowers. 'Alba' bears green leaves and tiny, white flowers. It is tolerant of extreme heat and drought. 'Rosea' has pink flowers.

O. regnellii is a vigorous, shade-loving species that has large foliage and dainty flowers. Watch for the CHARMED SERIES from Proven Winners.

O. vulcanicola is a small, bushy, spreading plant with reddish stems, green foliage flushed with red, and yellow flowers with purple-red veining. 'Copper Tones' and 'Molten Lava' have gold foliage with a touch of rust and buttery yellow flowers at the tips of reddish stems. 'Zinfandel,' a Proven Selection by Proven Winners, produces dark burgundy, almost black foliage and tiny, vivid yellow blooms.

Pansy
Viola

V. x wittrockiana cultivar with vinca, coral bells and dracaena

Pansies are one of the best cool-season plants available. Planted in fall, most will overwinter and bloom with early-spring bulbs. Or, start the container season with an all-pansy pot in a mix of colors. Work in Johnny-jump-ups as accents—the dainty flowers are multi-colored.

Growing

Pansies prefer **full sun** but tolerate partial shade. The potting mix should be **moist** and **well drained**. Fertilize every two weeks with quarter-strength fertilizer.

Pansies do best when the weather is cool and often die back completely in summer. Plants may rejuvenate in fall, but it is often easier to plant new ones.

Tips

Pansies make good companions for spring-flowering bulbs and primroses. A pot of

Features: blue, purple, red, orange, yellow, pink or white, bicolored or multi-colored flowers **Height:** 3–10" **Spread:** 6–12" **Hardiness:** zones 5–9; usually grown as an annual **Grow rating:** easy

V. x wittrockiana cultivar with calla lily (above)
V. x wittrockiana (below)

spring pansies set where you can see it from indoors will remind you that summer is just around the corner.

Recommended

V. cornuta (horned violet, viola) is a low-growing, spreading plant. The flowers are usually in shades of blue, purple or white. **Chalon Hybrids** bear ruffled, bicolored or multi-colored flowers in shades of blue, red, rose or white. **Sorbet Series** has a wide color range. Planted in fall, they flower until the ground freezes and may surprise you with another show in spring. **'Sorbet Yesterday, Today and Tomorrow'** bears flowers that open white and gradually turn purple as they mature.

V. tricolor (Johnny-jump-up) is a popular species. The flowers are purple, white and yellow, usually in combination, although several varieties have flowers in a single color, often purple.

V. x wittrockiana (pansy) comes in blue, purple, red, orange, yellow, pink or white, often multi-colored or with face-like markings. **'Antique Shades Mix'** offers pastel combinations of plum, yellow, apricot, rust and cream. **'Can Can Mix'** bears frilly flowers with ruffled edges in bicolored and multi-colored combinations of yellow, purple, red, white, pink and blue. **Imperial Series** includes plants that bear large flowers in a range of unique colors. **'Imperial Frosty Rose'** has flowers with deep rose pink centers that gradually pale to white near the edges of the petals.

Johnny-jump-ups self-seed prolifically and may turn up from year to year in not only the container they were growing in, but in other containers too.

Parsley
Petroselinum

P. crispum with others

The tightly curled leaves and bright green color of parsley fills in the spaces among other plants in combination containers. Keep the plants close to the house for easy picking to use in salads, recipes or as a garnish. Try a combination pot with several different herbs.

Growing

Parsley grows well in **full sun** or **partial shade**. The potting mix should be **humus rich, moist** and **well drained**. Fertilize every two weeks with quarter-strength fertilizer. Direct sow seeds because the plants resent transplanting.

Tips

Parsley is a good mixer plant for containers. Its bushy growth fills in quickly, and the bright green creates a good background for bright red, scarlet or orange flowers in particular.

Recommended

P. crispum forms a clump of bright green, divided leaves. This plant is a biennial but is usually grown as an annual because it is the leaves that are desired, not the flowers or seeds. Cultivars may have flat or curly leaves. Flat leaves are more flavorful and curly are more decorative. Dwarf cultivars are also available.

Parsley leaves make a tasty and nutritious addition to salads. Tear freshly picked leaves and add them to your mixed greens.

Features: clump-forming habit; attractive foliage **Height:** 8–24" **Spread:** 12–24" **Hardiness:** zones 5–8; biennial grown as an annual **Grow rating:** easy

Perilla
Perilla

P. 'Magellanica,' a Proven Selections plant from Proven Winners, and others

Growing

Perilla prefers **full sun** or **partial shade**. The potting mix should be **fertile, moist** and **well drained**. Soil amended with compost or well-composted manure is of added benefit. Plants can be pinched for more bushiness. Perilla may self-seed prolifically.

Tips

Perilla is a great thriller element in planters. It is the perfect alternative to coleus and is an ideal complement to brightly colored annuals and perennials in decorative containers.

Recommended

P. frutescens is a vigorous annual with deeply toothed, medium green, purple-flecked, cinnamon-lemon flavored leaves. Tiny, white flowers are borne on spikes in summer, but this annual is grown more for its ornate, colorful foliage. **'Atropurpurea'** (beefsteak plant) bears dark purple-red leaves. **Var. *crispa*** (var. *nankinensis*; 'Crispa') has dark bronze to purple foliage with very frilly leaf margins. **'Magilla'** ('Magilla Purple') bears multi-colored leaves of purple, green, white and pink, and **'Magilla Vanilla'** bears white and green leaves.

Perilla has been used for centuries as a medicinal plant in Chinese medicine and as an Asian culinary herb. Recently, breeders have introduced more decorative selections to the market, making perilla a highly sought-after plant.

Perilla is well known for its tolerance of summer heat and will easily compete with some of the most aggressive summer annuals available.

Also called: shiso, Chinese basil **Features:** bushy, vigorous habit; ornate, colorful foliage **Height:** 12–24" **Spread:** 12–24" **Hardiness:** annual **Grow rating:** easy

Periwinkle
Vinca

Periwinkle is one of the easiest plants to use in containers, spilling effortlessly over the rims of hanging baskets, window boxes and large mixed pots. Dark, evergreen leaves can last through winter on this vining perennial.

Growing

Grow periwinkle in **partial to full shade**. The potting mix should be evenly **moist** and **well drained**. Fertilize monthly during the growing season with quarter-strength fertilizer. Move containers to a sheltered location out of the wind in winter.

Tips

Periwinkle is a useful, attractive spiller plant for containers and hanging baskets. Poke a few rooted stems in here and there to provide a dark green background in your mixed containers.

Recommended

V. major (greater periwinkle) forms a low mat of trailing stems with glossy, dark green leaves. It bears purple or blue flowers and is often grown as an annual. **'Variegata'** has irregular, creamy margins on light green, glossy leaves. (Zones 6–9)

V. minor (lesser periwinkle) forms a low, loose mat of trailing stems and bears purple or blue flowers. **'Atropurpurea'** bears reddish purple flowers. **'Sterling Silver'** has cream-edged foliage and blue flowers.

Be careful to keep periwinkle in the pot—it roots easily and can become invasive in the landscape.

V. minor and *V. minor* 'Illumination' with geraniums

Also called: vinca **Features:** low, trailing, hardy or tender vine; blue-purple, pale blue, reddish purple or white, early- to mid-spring flowers; green or variegated, glossy foliage **Height:** 4–12" **Spread:** 2–4' **Hardiness:** zones 3–9 **Grow rating:** easy

Petunia

Petunia

P. x hybrida with English ivy and reed palm

The rekindling of interest in petunias resulted largely from the development of many exciting new varieties.

Features: bushy to trailing habit; summer flowers in shades of pink, blue, purple, red, yellow or white, or bicolored **Height:** 6–18"
Spread: 12–24" or wider **Hardiness:** annual
Grow rating: easy

Petunias come in so many styles that you can endlessly customize your containers. In addition to a wide range of colors, petunias can be trailing, cascading or spreading, grandiflora, multiflora or milliflora, often in both single-flowering and double-flowering varieties. Just supply the sunshine and enjoy them.

Growing

Petunias prefer **full sun**. The potting mix should be **well drained**. Fertilize no more than monthly with quarter-strength fertilizer. Pinch halfway back in mid-summer to keep plants bushy and to encourage new growth and flowers.

Tips

Planted alone, their bushy growth will fill a container and spill over the edge. The rich colors of their flowers also make them excellent companions for other annuals as well as for any container plantings of shrubs or small trees.

Recommended

P. x *hybrida* is a large group of popular, sun-loving annuals that fall into three categories: the grandifloras, with the largest flowers; the multifloras, bearing many medium-sized flowers; and the millifloras, with the smallest flowers.

P. **Storm Series** are grandiflora petunias that are weather and disease tolerant and bear large blooms in a range of colors.

P. **Supertunia Series** offers flowers in a wide range of pinks and purples, but there are also red, white and yellow selections.

P. **Wave Series** are vigorous, low-growing, spreading plants that bloom almost non-stop in a range of colors. They are tolerant of rain and cold. Look for 'Blue,' 'Pink,' 'Purple,' 'Misty Lilac,' 'Lavender' and 'Rose.' **Tidal Wave Series** are upright, spreading plants. Selections include 'Cherry,' 'Pink Hot,' 'Purple' and 'Silver.' **Easy Wave Series** are mound-forming petunias similar to the original Wave Series but a little taller. Easy Wave selections include 'Blue,' 'Coral Reef,' 'Mystic Pink,' 'Pink,' 'Red,' 'Rosy Dawn,' 'Salmon,' 'Shell Pink' and 'White.'

P. milliflora (above), *P.* Wave Series 'Lavender' (below)

The name Petunia *is derived from* petun, *the Brazilian word for tobacco, which comes from species of the related genus* Nicotiana.

Phormium
Phormium

P. tenax cultivar with echivaria and hens and chicks

Also called: New Zealand flax **Features:** clump-forming habit; green, black, red or yellow, often multi-colored and striped foliage **Height:** 2–8' **Spread:** 2–8' **Hardiness:** zones 9–10; tender perennial grown as an annual **Grow rating:** medium

The strappy leaves of phormium grow in V-shaped fans from the base of the plant.

Growing

Phormiums grow best in **full sun** but appreciate some protection from the hot afternoon sun. The potting mix should be **moist** and **well drained**. Fertilize every two weeks during the growing season with half-strength fertilizer. Plants can be overwintered in a bright, cool, frost-free location indoors. They may overwinter in protected areas outside in the southern Midwest.

Tips

Phormiums are great thriller plants in combination plantings, and even more thrilling as well-grown specimens. The bold and exotic foliage will draw the eye.

Recommended

P. hybrids are crosses of *P. cookianium* and *P. tenax*. **'Jester'** has bright pink-red foliage with light green margins. **'Pink Flamingo'** has dark green foliage that has abundant pink and dark pink variegations. **'Rainbow Queen'** ('Maori Queen') bears bronze-green foliage with rosy red stripes. **'Sundowner'** has broad, upright, light bronzy green foliage margined with pink and yellow. **'Yellow Wave'** bears yellow-green leaves striped with darker green.

P. tenax (New Zealand flax) forms a large clump of long, stiff, dark green leaves with gray-green undersides. **'Aurora'** has bronzy green leaves striped with pink, yellow and red. **'Pink Stripe'** has pink-edged, dark gray-green to dark bronze-green foliage. **'Purpureum'** (*P. atropurpureum*; Purpureum Group) has upright, dark purple foliage.

Piggyback Plant
Tolmiea

T. menziesii

Piggyback plant's mounded leaves are weighed down by newly produced foliage, creating a cascading appearance. It is often grown as a houseplant.

Growing

Piggyback plant grows best in **full shade**, **light shade** or **partial shade** with protection from the hot afternoon sun. The potting mix should be **moist** and **well drained**. Fertilize monthly during the growing season with quarter-strength fertilizer. Where they are not hardy, keep plants in a cool, bright room in winter. Where they are hardy, move plants to a sheltered location protected from temperature fluctuations.

Tips

The unique way of producing new plantlets from the surface of an existing leaf makes this tender perennial a fine addition to shady hanging baskets. It can also be grown in containers where you can observe the intriguing foliage from above. Piggyback plant is an ideal addition to an understory-themed container or for a container on a heavily shaded balcony.

Recommended

T. menziesii is a clump-forming plant with hairy, heart-shaped leaves with toothed edges. Small plantlets emerge where the leaf and stem join. Tiny, tubular, greenish, insignificant flowers open along one side of the leaf. **'Variegata'** has yellow-splashed leaves, and **'Taff's Gold'** produces both solid and variegated leaves.

Features: clump-forming habit; decorative, piggyback foliage **Height:** 12–18" **Spread:** 12–18" **Hardiness:** zones 6–9; perennial grown as an annual **Grow rating:** easy

Plectranthus
Plectranthus

P. ciliatus 'Vanilla Twist,' a Proven Winners Selection, with sedge, purple fountain grass, English ivy and coleus

The trailing stems root easily from cuttings; start some in late summer to grow indoors through winter.

Features: bushy to trailing habit; decorative foliage **Height:** 8–12" **Spread:** about 36" **Hardiness:** annual; tender perennial grown as an annual **Grow rating:** easy

These mound-forming plants, with their often-aromatic foliage, eventually develop a more trailing habit. They are drought and heat tolerant and don't typically flower. Many cultivars have reddish to burgundy stems contrasting with lime green foliage often speckled with white.

Growing

Plectranthus grows best in **light shade** or **partial shade**. The potting mix should be **moist** and **well drained**. Fertilize every two weeks with quarter- to half-strength fertilizer.

Tips

These trailing plants make fabulous fillers for hanging baskets and mixed containers. Place them near a walkway or other area where people will be able to brush past the plants and smell the spicy-scented foliage.

Recommended

P. argentatus is an upright to spreading plant with silvery green, hairy stems and leaves. It bears clusters of small, bluish white flowers near the ends of stems in summer.

P. ciliatus is a low-growing, trailing plant with burgundy stems and lilac blue flowers. The dark to olive green, toothed foliage has burgundy undersides. 'Vanilla Twist' has bright green leaves with white, scalloped margins.

P. coleoides 'Frosted Jade' has green and white variegated foliage on pink stems.

P. forsteri is a mounding then trailing plant with light green, slightly hairy leaves and clusters of small, white or pale purple flowers in summer. 'Marginatus' has cream-edged leaves.

Purple Fountain Grass

Pennisetum

P. setaceum BURGUNDY GIANT with euphorbia, mondo grass, coleus, English ivy and dwarf plumbago

Purple fountain grass is a low-maintenance plant, even in a container. It has a graceful, soft but also bold form that makes it a striking companion to flowering plants.

Growing

Purple fountain grass grows best in **full sun**. The potting mix should be **well drained**. Fertilize monthly during the growing season with quarter-strength

Winter interest is a feature of ornamental grasses—the plants turn a tan color and continue to stand even through snow.

Features: arching or upright habit; decorative foliage; fuzzy, pink, purple or tan, summer and fall flowers **Height:** 1–6'
Spread: 18"–4' **Hardiness:** zones 6–10; tender perennial grown as an annual
Grow rating: easy

P. setaceum 'Rubrum' (above)
P. glaucum 'Purple Majesty' with others (below)

fertilizer. Where hardy, keep purple fountain grass in a sheltered location out of the wind and sun and protected from temperature fluctuations in winter. Where not hardy, it can be cut back in fall and stored in a cool location indoors or treated as an annual.

Tips

Purple fountain grass makes an interesting alternative to dracaena and spike in mixed containers. The colorful foliage can be used to accent color-themed containers.

Recommended

P. alopecuriodes forms clumps of long, narrow, bright green, arching leaves. Soft spikes of tan, pink or purple, fuzzy flowers are produced on long, arching stems in summer and fall. **'Hameln'** is a dwarf cultivar hardy to zone 5. **'Little Bunny'** is an even smaller selection that grows only 12" tall. (Zones 6–9)

P. glaucum **'Purple Majesty'** (purple majesty millet, ornamental millet) has a corn-like growth habit, with a strong central stalk and broad, blackish purple, strap-like leaves. The bottlebrush-like flower spikes are also purple, though the tiny flowers may be yellow. (Zones 8–10)

P. setaceum **'Rubrum'** ('Purpureum'; annual fountain grass) is a dense, mound forming, tender perennial grass that is grown as an annual. It has narrow, dark purple foliage and large, showy, rose red flower spikes from mid-summer to fall. BURGUNDY GIANT, a Proven Selection by Proven Winners, has wider, deep burgundy foliage. Its nodding flower spikes are pinkish purple. (Zones 9–10)

Rose
Rosa

R. 'Knock Out' (above & below)

America's favorite flower should be included in the container garden, whether you limit yourself to the miniatures or venture into some of the standard-sized types, which will eventually need to be moved to the garden.

Growing

Roses grow best in **full sun**. The potting mix should be **humus rich, slightly acidic, moist** and **well drained**. Fertilize every two weeks during the growing season with half-strength fertilizer. Deadhead lightly to keep plants tidy and to encourage prolific blooming, except roses such as 'Knock Out,' which develop attractive hips after the flowers are done.

Features: rounded to arching shrub; often-fragrant, mid-summer to fall flowers **Height:** 1–4' **Spread:** 1–4' **Hardiness:** zones 3–9 **Grow rating:** medium

R. 'Hansa' (above), R. 'Cupcake' (below)

Tips

Bushy modern shrub roses, miniature roses and hardy roses are the best choices for containers. The miniatures make good companions for mixed containers, while the larger, shrubbier roses make good focal points, perhaps with white-flowered, trailing plants such as bacopas planted around them.

Recommended

R. **'Cupcake'** is a compact, bushy miniature shrub rose with glossy, green foliage. It produces clusters of light to medium pink flowers all summer. It grows 12–18" tall, with an equal spread. (Zones 5–9)

R. **'Knock Out'** has an attractive, rounded form with glossy, green leaves that turn to shades of burgundy in fall. The bright, cherry red flowers are borne in clusters almost all summer and fall. Orange-red hips last well into winter. It grows about 4' tall and wide and is disease resistant. Several colors and a double-flowering cultivar are now available. (Zones 4–9)

R. **'Rise 'n' Shine'** is a popular miniature selection that works beautifully in containers and along the edge of raised beds and planters. It bears clusters of medium yellow blooms that have unusual, quill-like petals that arise from hybrid tea-like buds.

Miniature roses can be overwintered indoors in a cool, bright room.

Rosemary
Rosmarinus

These pretty little evergreens have fragrant foliage and varied habits that make them worth growing whether you have an herb collection or not.

Growing

Rosemary prefers **full sun** but tolerates partial shade. The potting mix should be evenly **moist** and **well drained**; this plant doesn't like wet soil but doesn't like to dry out completely either. Fertilize no more than once a month during the growing season with quarter-strength fertilizer. This tender shrub must be moved indoors in winter and kept in the brightest location available.

Tips

Rosemary can be grown in a container as a specimen or with other plants. Low-growing, spreading plants can be grown in hanging baskets.

Recommended

R. officinalis is a dense, bushy, evergreen shrub with narrow, dark green leaves. The habit varies somewhat among cultivars from strongly upright to prostrate and spreading. Flowers are usually in shades of blue, but pink-flowered cultivars are available.

R. officinalis 'Prostratus'

To keep plants bushy, pinch the tips back. The bits you pinch off can be used to flavor roast chicken, soups and stews.

Features: evergreen shrub; attractive, fragrant foliage; bright blue, sometimes pink, summer flowers **Height:** 8"–4' **Spread:** 1–4' **Hardiness:** zones 8–10; overwintered indoors **Grow rating:** easy

Rush

Juncus

J. effusus 'Spiralis' with impatiens

Rushes, particularly the curly- or spiral-leaved cultivars, are popular, eye-catching plants that provide a different way to extend height in a combination container. Grow them with other moisture-loving plants such as iris and sedge.

Growing

Rushes grow well in **full sun** or **partial shade**. The potting mix should be **acidic** and **moist to wet**. Fertilize no more than monthly during the growing season with quarter-strength fertilizer. Where plants are hardy, move containers to a sheltered location protected from temperature fluctuations in winter. Grow them as annuals where they aren't hardy.

Features: marginally aquatic perennial; decorative, stem-like leaves **Height:** 18–24" **Spread:** 12" **Hardiness:** zones 4–8 **Grow rating:** easy

Tips

Rushes can be grown in shallow, gravel-filled water dishes, where they can be used to create a unique, living centerpiece for your patio table.

Recommended

J. effusus (soft rush) forms a tufted clump of long, flexible, stem-like leaves and bears insignificant flowers in summer. The species is rarely grown. **'Spiralis'** (corkscrew rush) forms a tangled mass of curling, corkscrew-like leaves. **'Variegated Spiral Rush'** has white-streaked leaves. (Zones 6–8)

J. inflexus (hard rush) forms a clump of stiff, stem-like leaves. **'Afro'** has more tightly spiraled stems than 'Spiralis.'

Rushes are "marginals" to a pond gardener, meaning they like their feet wet at the edge of water.

Salvia
Salvia

Proven Winners Selection *S. officinalis* 'Purpurea' with African daisy, sedge and others

alvias are both annual and perennial, but most container gardeners choose the annual varieties. The herb variety is great in a kitchen container. Most have aromatic foliage—try pineapple sage, an aptly named variety with tiny, red flowers late in the season.

Growing

Salvias grow best in **full sun** but tolerate light shade. The potting mix should be **humus rich, moist** and **well drained**. Fertilize every two weeks during the

Sage has been used since at least ancient Greek times as a medicinal and culinary herb and continues to be widely used for both those purposes today.

Also called: sage **Features:** bushy habit; decorative, sometimes fragrant foliage; red, blue, purple, lavender, burgundy, plum, pink, orange, salmon, yellow, cream, white or bicolored, summer flowers **Height:** 12–24"
Spread: 8–24" **Hardiness:** zones 4–10; tender perennial grown as an annual
Grow rating: easy

growing season with quarter- to half-strength fertilizer. Move containers to a sheltered location protected from temperature fluctuations in winter. Salvias are often treated like annuals where they won't survive winter.

Tips

Use salvias as fillers or as specimens for their outstanding foliage-flower combinations. Use common sage with other edible herbs such as rosemary, basil and thyme for a fragrant, edible container.

Recommended

S. farinacea (blue sage, mealy cup sage) has bright blue flowers clustered along stems powdered with silver. **'Victoria'** is a popular cultivar with silvery foliage and deep blue flowers. (Zones 8–10)

S. greggii (autumn sage) is a compact, shrubby perennial. It bears red, pink, purple or yellow flowers. **'Raspberry Royale'** bears raspberry red flowers. (Zones 7–9)

S. officinalis is a woody, mounding plant with soft, gray-green leaves. It bears light purple flowers in early and mid-summer. Many attractive cultivars are available, including the silver-leaved **'Berggarten,'** the purple-leaved **'Purpurea,'** the yellow-margined **'Icterina'** and the green and cream variegated **'Tricolor,'** which has a pink flush to the new growth. (Zones 4–8)

S. splendens (salvia, scarlet sage) is a bushy perennial grown as an annual. It bears bright red flowers. Recently, cultivars have become available in white, pink, purple or orange. **'Salsa'** bears solid and bicolored flowers in shades of red, orange, purple, burgundy, cream or pink. **Sizzler Series** bears flowers in burgundy, lavender, pink, plum, red, salmon, or white and salmon bicolored.

S. splendens 'Sizzler White' with basil (above)
S. officinalis 'Icterina' (below)

Scarlet Runner Bean
Phaseolus

Scarlet runner bean is a vine that clambers up a support for a vertical element and provides edible, green beans. If you're ready for something a bit more exotic, try hyacinth bean (*Lablab purpureus*). It has flashier pink-purple flowers and burgundy bean pods but is not as easily prepared as a vegetable.

Growing

Scarlet runner bean grows best in **full sun**. The potting mix should be **moist** and **well drained**. Fertilize monthly with quarter- to half-strength fertilizer. This plant should be placed near something it can twine around. A porch railing or obelisk is suitable.

Tips

Scarlet runner bean has a carefree habit, twisting and twining around any structure you can provide for it. It does well in a container with an obelisk-type frame to climb. Create a similar look simply by poking three or four long poles into the container and tying them together at the top. Plant scarlet runner bean in a hanging basket for a unique display.

Recommended

P. coccineus is a twining, annual vine. Scarlet red flowers are borne in clusters in summer, followed by long, edible pods. **Var. *alba*** (Dutch runner bean) bears white flowers. **'Painted Lady'** bears red and white bicolored flowers.

P. coccineus

The edible, dark green pods are tender when young and are best eaten before they become stringy and tough.

Features: twining vine; red, white or bicolored, summer flowers; edible fruit **Height:** 6–8' **Spread:** 1–6' **Hardiness:** annual **Grow rating:** easy

Sedge
Carex

C. buchananii, from Proven Winners,
with argyranthemum and others

*Sedges are native to moist wetlands. In
the wild, their dense, tufted clumps can
mislead hikers into believing the ground
is more solid than it is.*

Features: tuft-forming perennial; interesting,
colorful foliage; attractive habit **Height:** 1–4'
Spread: 1–4' **Hardiness:** zones 5–9
Grow rating: medium

With its green, blue, rust, bronze
or gold foliage, sedge allows gardeners to add broad, colorful strokes or
bright accents to their containers. Grow
it with other moisture-loving plants.

Growing

Sedges grow well in **full sun** or **partial
shade**. The potting mix should be **neutral to slightly alkaline** and **moist to
wet**. 'Frosted Curls' needs normal moisture and should not be overwatered.
Fertilize every two weeks during the

growing season with quarter-strength fertilizer. Move plants to an unheated shed or garage where they will be protected from temperature fluctuations in winter, or grow them as annuals.

Tips

Sedges offer colorful foliage and rustic texture to contrast with other moisture-loving plants. The cascading habit of many of these grass-like plants makes them an interesting choice to grow as specimens in containers. 'Frosted Curls' contrasts well with coarse-textured plants.

Recommended

C. buchananii (leatherleaf sedge) forms a dense clump or tuft of narrow, arching, orange-brown leaves. (Zones 6–9)

C. comans 'Frosted Curls' (New Zealand hair sedge) is a compact, clump-forming, evergreen perennial with fine-textured, pale green, weeping foliage. The foliage appears almost iridescent, with unusual curled and twisted tips. (Zones 7–9)

C. elata 'Aurea' (Bowles' golden sedge) forms a clump of arching, grass-like, yellow leaves with green edges. It bears spikes of tiny, brown or green flowers in early summer.

C. morrowii 'Aureovariegata' (variegated Japanese sedge) forms low tufts of drooping, green-and-yellow-striped foliage. (Zones 6–9)

C. pendula (drooping sedge, weeping sedge) forms a clump of graceful, arching, grass-like, green leaves. Drooping spikes of brown flowers are borne on long stems in late spring and early summer.

C. comans 'Frosted Curls' (right)

Sedum
Sedum

Sedum with lavender

Many sedums are grown for their foliage, which can range in color from steel gray-blue and green to red and burgundy.

Also called: stonecrop **Features:** mat-forming or upright perennial; yellow, white, red or pink, summer to fall flowers; decorative, fleshy foliage **Height:** 2–24" **Spread:** 12–24" **Hardiness:** zones 3–9 **Grow rating:** easy

Sedums can be grown in low, wide dishes to be placed on a stairway so that they cascade over the edge of the dish and down the stairs. The flowers are an added bonus.

Growing
Sedums prefer **full sun** but tolerate partial shade. The potting mix should be **neutral to alkaline** and **very well drained**. Fertilize no more than once a month during the growing season with half-strength fertilizer. Early-summer pruning of upright species and hybrids encourages compact, bushy growth but can delay flowering. Move containers to a sheltered location protected from temperature fluctuations in winter.

Tips
Low-growing sedums make wonderful filler plants for mixed containers, where many will grow over the edge of the pot. Taller selections make good contrast plants for mixed containers.

Recommended
S. acre (gold moss stonecrop) is a low-growing, wide-spreading plant that bears small, yellow-green flowers.

S. spectabile (showy stonecrop) is an upright perennial species with pink flowers. Cultivars are available. Most are relatively large plants.

S. spurium (two-row stonecrop) forms a low, wide mat of foliage with deep pink or white flowers. Many cultivars are available and are often grown for their colorful foliage.

Snapdragon
Antirrhinum

Snapdragons have been popular for many years because of their unique blooms. Grow them in containers for their fragrance, the length of their bloom time and their ability to withstand cooler temperatures.

Growing
Snapdragons prefer **full sun** but tolerate light shade or partial shade. The potting mix should be **humus rich, neutral to alkaline** and **well drained**. Fertilize every two weeks during the growing season with quarter- to half-strength fertilizer. To encourage bushier growth, pinch the tips of young plants. Cut off the flower spikes as they fade to promote further blooming.

Tips
Snapdragons look lovely planted alone or in mixed containers. There is even a trailing variety that does well in hanging baskets. The strong, upright, vividly colored flower spikes contrast beautifully with arching grasses and broad, leafy plants.

Recommended
A. majus is a bushy, clump-forming plant from which flower spikes emerge in summer. Many cultivars are available in dwarf (up to 12" tall), medium (12–24" tall) and giant (up to 4' tall) sizes. **'Floral Showers'** grows 6–8" tall and bears flowers in a wide range of solid colors and bicolors. **'Lampion'** has a trailing habit and cascades up to 36". **'Black Prince'** grows 18" tall and bears striking, dark purple-red flowers with bronzy green foliage. **Rocket Series** cultivars have good heat tolerance, grow to 4' tall and produce long spikes of brightly colored flowers in many shades.

A. *majus* cultivar

Snapdragons are interesting and long lasting in fresh flower arrangements. The buds continue to mature and open long after the spike has been cut.

Features: clump-forming habit; white, cream, yellow, orange, red, maroon, pink, purple or bicolored, summer flowers; glossy, green to bronze foliage **Height:** 6"–4' **Spread:** 6–12" **Hardiness:** tender perennial grown as an annual **Grow rating:** easy

Spider Flower
Cleome

C. hassleriana with nicotiana, geranium and impatiens

Not the daintiest of plants, spider flower shoots upward with spiny stems and unremarkable foliage. Then come the flower heads, which are colorful, structurally unique and remarkable for seed production. If your container is in or near a flowerbed, watch for seedlings the next year—they are almost a guarantee.

Growing

Spider flower prefers **full sun** but tolerates partial shade. The potting mix should be **moist** and **well drained**. These plants are drought tolerant but look and perform best if watered regularly. Fertilize monthly with quarter-strength fertilizer. Pinch out the center of the plant when transplanting, and it will branch out to produce up to a dozen blooms. Deadhead to prolong the blooming period.

Tips

Spider flower is an interesting plant to use as the central or focal plant in a mixed container.

Recommended

C. hassleriana is a tall, upright plant with strong, supple, thorny stems. The foliage and flowers have a strong but pleasant scent. Flowers are borne in loose, rounded clusters at the ends of leafy stems. Many cultivars are available. **'Helen Campbell'** has white flowers. **Royal Queen Series** bears fade-resistant flowers in all colors. **'Sparkler Blush'** is a dwarf cultivar that grows up to 36" tall. It bears pink flowers that fade to white.

C. serrulata (Rocky Mountain bee plant) is native to western North America. It is rarely available commercially. The thornless dwarf cultivar **'Solo'** is available to be grown from seed. It grows 12–18" tall and bears pink and white blooms.

Features: bushy, upright habit; scented, divided foliage; pink, rose, violet or white flower clusters **Height:** 1–5' **Spread:** 18–36" **Hardiness:** annual **Grow rating:** easy

Spider Plant
Chlorophytum

Spider plant grows quickly and produces flowers and stems of little plantlets while still quite young. The grass-like, narrow leaf blades arch gracefully as they grow, creating a spider-like effect. Long, trailing stems cascade over the pot's edge and carry small plantlets that resemble dangling baby spiders.

Growing

Spider plant grows best in **light shade** or **partial shade** with protection from the hot afternoon sun. The potting mix should be **moist** and **well drained**. The plant is fairly drought tolerant. Fertilize every two weeks during the growing season with quarter-strength fertilizer. Spider plant can be moved indoors in winter, but it is often easier to snip off a few of the baby plantlets and grow those over winter to use the following spring.

Tips

This houseplant staple can be used as a filler plant for mixed containers. The green or variegated leaves brighten up a container shared with darker-leaved plants such as coral bells and begonia.

Recommended

C. comosum forms a clump of graceful, arching, grass-like leaves. Flowering stems emerge from the rosette bearing tiny, white flowers and young plantlets. The stems are pendant, weighed down by the plantlets. **'Milky Way'** has creamy leaf margins. **'Variegatum'** has cream to white leaf margins. **'Vittatum'** has leaves with a white central stripe and green margins.

C. comosum and *C. comosum* 'Vittatum'

Spider plants are incredibly adaptable, tolerating a wide range of conditions including heat or cold, sun or shade and humid or dry air.

Features: clump-forming habit; decorative, arching, strap-like foliage; stems of trailing or dangling plantlets **Height:** 12" **Spread:** 24–36" **Hardiness:** tender perennial grown as an annual or overwintered indoors **Grow rating:** easy

Spike
Cordyline

C. australis

Spike can tolerate heat and drought, but it is sensitive to fluoride in the soil or water.

Also called: cabbage palm, cabbage tree
Features: erect to arching foliage **Height:** 3–10' **Spread:** 3–5' **Hardiness:** zones 8–11; often grown as an annual **Grow rating:** easy

Spike is the standard for a vertical element in a combination container. It will grow all season without problems. Scour garden centers for one of the cultivars below to vary the routine and customize your containers.

Growing
Spike grows best in **full sun** or **partial shade**. Purple-leaved varieties exhibit their best color in full sun, while the variegated selections prefer partial shade. The planting mix should be **moist, fertile** and **well drained**, with lots of compost mixed in. Feed monthly during the growing season with half-strength fertilizer. If you bring your plant indoors in winter, place it in a bright, sunny location and reduce watering.

Tips
Spike develops a taproot with age, so choose a large, deep container if you intend to keep the plant for a few years.

Recommended
C. australis (*Dracaena indivisa*) is an upright plant with erect to arching, medium to light green foliage. The leaves are 12–36" long and 1–2" wide. Young plants exhibit a fountain-like form. A trunk will develop over many years of growth. **'Lemon Fountain'** has green leaves irregularly striped with yellow. **'Purple Tower'** is a hybrid that has wide, plum purple to dark purple leaves. **'Red Sensation'** has narrow, bronze-purple foliage. **'Red Star'** has bronze-tinged burgundy foliage. **'Sundance'** has green leaves with a red main vein. **'Torbay Dazzler'** bears creamy white leaves irregularly striped with green.

Spruce
Picea

Dwarf spruces are well suited to container growing, bringing their evergreen foliage and upright stature to the deck or patio year-round.

Growing

Spruce trees grow best in **full sun.** The potting mix should be **neutral to acidic, moist** and **well drained.** Be sure to plant them in the biggest container you can so that they won't tip over. Fertilize monthly during the growing season with quarter-strength fertilizer. Move containers to a sheltered location protected from the sun and wind in winter. Replant in the garden after three to five years.

Tips

With many intriguing shapes and colors, spruces make fine architectural elements in a container setting. Plant dwarf and slow-growing spruce cultivars with drought-tolerant plants in mixed containers, because spruces tend to quickly consume the available moisture.

Recommended

P. abies (Norway spruce) is a tall, upright, pyramidal tree, but it has many dwarf cultivars. **'Little Gem'** is a slow-growing, rounded cultivar. **'Nidiformis'** (nest spruce) is a slow-growing, low, compact, mounding plant. **Forma pendula** are variable, weeping or prostrate forms of spruce. Staked at about 4', they develop into beautiful weeping specimens.

P. glauca **var.** *albertiana* **'Conica'** (dwarf Alberta spruce) is a slow-growing, dense, conical, bushy shrub. Its needles may scorch in too windy or hot a location. **'Jean's Dilly'** is a smaller selection with shorter, thinner needles and twisted branch ends.

P. glauca var. albertiana 'Conica'

Spruces frequently produce branch mutations, and it is often from these that the dwarf selections are developed.

Features: conical or columnar, evergreen tree or shrub; attractive foliage; varied habit **Height:** 2–6' **Spread:** 2–4' **Hardiness:** zones 2–8 **Grow rating:** medium

Swan River Daisy
Brachyscome (Brachycome)

B. iberidifolia BLUE ZEPHYR

This plant's dainty, daisy-like flowers and lacy, fern-like foliage make a winning combination. Newer cultivars introduce pink, lavender and deep purple flowers to the lineup that was traditionally white.

Growing

Swan River daisy prefers **full sun** but benefits from light shade in the afternoon. The potting mix should be **well drained**. Allow the soil to dry between waterings. Fertilize once a month with half-strength fertilizer. Plant early because cool spring weather encourages compact, sturdy growth. This frost-tolerant plant dies back when summer gets too hot. If it fades, cut it back and move it to a slightly shadier spot.

Tips

Plant this versatile annual near the edges of mixed containers and hanging baskets so that its bushy growth will hang over the sides and its little flowers will poke through its neighbors' leaves.

Recommended

B. iberidifolia forms a bushy, spreading mound. Blue-purple or pink-purple, daisy-like flowers are borne all summer. BLUE ZEPHYR, a Proven Selection from Proven Winners, is a heat-tolerant cultivar that will bloom all season. '**Hot Candy**' bears heat-tolerant, dark pink flowers that fade to pale pink. '**Toucan Tango**' has heat-tolerant, mauve flowers with lime green centers.

Features: mounding or spreading habit; blue, pink, white or purple, summer flowers, usually with yellow centers; feathery foliage **Height:** 6–18" **Spread:** 8–24" **Hardiness:** annual **Grow rating:** medium

Sweet Alyssum
Lobularia

Sweet alyssum is an excellent plant for softening the edges of container plantings, and it should not be ignored when planting a fragrance garden. Just a few plants can fill your garden with a sweet, honey-like scent.

Growing

Sweet alyssum prefers **full sun** but tolerates light shade. The potting mix should be **well drained** and **moist**. Fertilize monthly with quarter- to half-strength fertilizer. Sweet alyssum may die back a bit during hot and humid summers. Trim it back and ensure the potting mix remains moist to encourage new growth and more flowers when the weather cools.

Tips

Sweet alyssum is good for filling in spaces between taller plants in mixed containers. It will self-seed, sometimes quite a bit, and you may have seedlings popping up in other containers and odd areas in your garden and landscape.

Recommended

L. maritima forms a low, spreading mound of foliage. The entire plant appears to be covered in tiny blossoms when in full flower. Cultivars are available in a range of flower colors.

L. maritima with pineapple lily

Leave sweet alyssum plants alone through winter. In spring, remove last year's growth to expose the self-sown seedlings below.

Features: fragrant flowers in pink, purple, yellow, salmon or white **Height:** 3–12" **Spread:** 6–24" **Hardiness:** annual **Grow rating:** easy

Sweet Flag
Acorus

A. gramineus 'Ogon'

These plants are much admired for their habit as well as for the wonderful, spicy fragrance of the crushed leaves.

Growing

Sweet flags grow best in **full sun**. The potting mix should be **moist to wet**. Fertilize monthly during the growing season with quarter- to half-strength fertilizer. Move containers to a sheltered location such as an unheated shed or garage in winter.

Tips

Include sweet flags, with their glossy, often striped leaves, in a mixed container with plants such as calla lilies and elephant ears for an attractive, texturally intriguing, moisture loving container.

Recommended

A. calamus (sweet flag) is a large, clump-forming plant with long, narrow, bright green, fragrant foliage. **'Variegatus'** has vertically striped yellow, cream and green leaves.

A. gramineus (dwarf sweet flag, Japanese rush) forms low, fan-shaped clumps of fragrant, glossy, green, narrow leaves. **'Minimus Aureus'** is a very low-growing cultivar with bright golden yellow leaves. **'Ogon,'** a Proven Selection from Proven Winners, has cream-and-green-striped leaves. **'Pusillus'** (dwarf Japanese rush) is another low-growing cultivar. (Zones 5–11)

Features: clump-forming perennial; narrow, stiff or arching, grass-like, sometimes variegated leaves; moisture loving **Height:** 4"–5' **Spread:** 4–24" **Hardiness:** zones 4–11 **Grow rating:** medium

The roots have a sweet fragrance, and they were once used to flavor candy.

Sweet Potato Vine

Ipomoea

I. batatas BLACK HEART, from Proven Winners

Sweet potato vine is just one of the spillers in a genus that also includes moonflower and morning glory. Sweet potato vine produces large leaves in unique colors. Moonflower is so named for its night-opening blooms with a sweet fragrance. Morning glory is an annual vine with large, often blue blooms that can cover a trellis.

Grow moonflower on a porch or on a trellis near a patio that is used in the evening so that the sweetly scented flowers can be fully enjoyed.

Features: twining climber; white, blue, pink or purple flowers; sometimes variegated or colorful foliage **Height:** 1–10' **Spread:** 12–24" **Hardiness:** annual; tender perennial grown as an annual **Grow rating:** easy

I. batatas 'Margarita' with coleus, English ivy, lamium and others (above), *I. batatas* 'Margarita' with juniper, coral bells and bamboo grass (below)

Growing

Ipomoea species grow well in **full sun**. The potting mix should be **light** and **well drained**. Fertilize sweet potato vine once a month during the growing season with quarter- to half-strength fertilizer. Other ipomoeas will bloom poorly if over-fertilized.

Tips

Sweet potato vines make excellent filler and accent plants in planters and hanging baskets. Morning glories and moonflowers will grow up small trellises.

Recommended

I. alba (moonflower) is a twining, perennial climber with heart-shaped leaves and sweetly scented, white flowers that open only at night. It prefers hot summers and will not begin blooming until late in the year in northern areas. Its tendrils become very woody by the end of summer, and it can be a problem to get the vines off trellises.

I. batatas (sweet potato vine) is a twining, perennial climber that is usually treated as a bushy or trailing plant rather than a climber. It is grown for its attractive foliage rather than its flowers. BLACK HEART, a Proven Selection by Proven Winners, has heart shaped, dark purple foliage. **'Blackie'** has dark purple (almost black), deeply lobed leaves. **'Margarita'** has yellow-green foliage on a fairly compact plant. **'Tricolor'** is a compact plant with light green, cream and bright pink variegated leaves.

I. purpurea (morning glory) is a twining, annual climber with heart-shaped leaves and purple, pink, blue or white, trumpet-shaped flowers.

I. tricolor (morning glory) is a twining, annual climber with heart-shaped, purple or blue flowers with white throats. **'Heavenly Blue'** bears sky blue flowers with white centers.

Thyme
Thymus

Use the groundcover type of thyme as a filler or spiller in combination planters, or grow the culinary type in combination with basil and other herbs in a kitchen container. Both kinds are somewhat hardy in containers.

Growing
Thyme prefers **full sun**. The potting mix should be **humus rich** and **very well drained**. Mix in compost or earthworm castings. These plants are fairly drought tolerant. Fertilize no more than monthly during the growing season with quarter-strength fertilizer. Move containers to a sheltered location protected from temperature fluctuations in winter.

Tips
Thyme is a nice addition to your herb collection. It can also be used at the edge of a mixed container, where the tiny leaves will soften the appearance of coarser-leaved companions.

Recommended
T. x *citriodorus* (lemon-scented thyme) forms a tidy, rounded mound of lemon-scented foliage and pale pink flowers. **'Argenteus'** has silver-edged leaves. **'Golden King'** has yellow-margined leaves. (Zones 5–9)

T. serpyllum (mother of thyme, wild thyme) is a low, creeping, mat-forming plant. It bears purple flowers. **'Elfin'** forms tiny, dense mounds of foliage. It rarely flowers. **'Minimalist'** ('Minimus') is lower growing than the species and bears pink flowers. **'Snowdrift'** has white flowers.

T. vulgaris (common thyme) forms a bushy mound of dark green leaves. The flowers may be purple, pink or white. **'Silver Posie'** has pale pink flowers and silver-edged leaves. (Zones 4–9)

T. x *citriodorus* 'Golden King' with parsley, rosemary and others

In the Middle Ages, people believed that drinking a thyme infusion would enable them to see fairies.

Features: mounding or creeping perennial; purple, pink or white, late-spring to early-summer flowers; tiny, fuzzy or glossy, often fragrant foliage **Height:** 2–18" **Spread:** 4–16" **Hardiness:** zones 3–9 **Grow rating:** easy

Tropical Hibiscus
Hibiscus

H. rosa-sinensis (above and bottom right)

Tropical hibiscus is an easy impulse purchase at the garden center. It can grow rather large over the season and may need some pruning and especially dead-heading to keep flowers forming. It is often brought indoors as a houseplant.

Growing
Tropical hibiscus grows well in **full sun, light shade** or **partial shade** with some protection from the hottest afternoon sun. The planting mix should be **moist** and **well drained**, with lots of compost mixed in. Tropical hibiscus appreciates humidity. Bring plants indoors before the first frost and place in a bright location with reduced watering over winter. Repot when necessary.

Tips
Tropical hibiscus is best used as a specimen, whether it is in shrub or standard form. Its yellow blooms with reddish throats make it a top-notch addition to any patio, deck or poolside.

Recommended
H. rosa-sinensis is a dense, rounded shrub that can grow 6' tall. It bears deep, dark green, oval-shaped, coarsely toothed, evergreen foliage that is 6" long. The single, semi-double or double flowers are 4–6" wide and come in shades of red, orange, yellow, white, pink or apricot. They remain open for only one day but are often produced in succession for long periods.

Tropical hibiscus is sometimes not fond of interior conditions and is known to completely defoliate.

Also called: rose of China **Features:** large, exotic flowers with prominent stamens; attractive foliage; good form **Height:** 3–6' **Spread:** 12–36" **Hardiness:** tender shrub grown as an annual **Grow rating:** medium

Verbena

Verbena

Verbena forms a dense mat of foliage with flowers in clusters at the end of its stems.

Growing

Verbena grows best in **full sun**. The potting mix should be **very well drained**. Fertilize every two weeks in summer with half-strength fertilizer. Pinch young plants back to encourage bushy growth. This plant will need to be deadheaded to keep the blooms coming.

Tips

Use verbena as a filler in large mixed containers and as a spiller in hanging baskets and window boxes. It is a good substitute for ivy geranium where the sun is hot and where a roof overhang keeps this mildew-prone plant dry.

Recommended

V. x *hybrida* is a bushy plant that may be upright or spreading. It bears clusters of small flowers in shades of white, purple, blue, pink, red, salmon, coral or yellow. **Babylon Series** is a group of compact, bushy plants with flowers in shades of deep or light blue, bright or light pink, dark or light purple, red or white. **'Peaches and Cream'** is a spreading plant with flowers that open soft peachy pink and fade to white. SUPERBENA SERIES, from Proven Winners, is a group of mounding then cascading, mildew-resistant plants with large, vividly colored flowers in shades of purple, burgundy, coral, red, pink or blue.

V. SUPERBENA DARK BLUE with salvia and euphorbia

To rejuvenate foliage and encourage more blooms, cut back the plants by half in mid-summer.

Features: mounding to cascading habit; red, pink, coral, purple, burgundy, blue or white flowers, sometimes with white centers **Height:** 8–24" **Spread:** 12–24" **Hardiness:** tender perennial grown as an annual **Grow rating:** easy

Vinca
Catharanthus

C. roseus

Compact, spreading plants produce relatively large blooms, often with a white eye, for most of summer. Many colors are available in this reliable annual.

Growing

Grow vinca in **full sun** or **partial shade**. The potting mix should be evenly **moist** and **well drained**. Fertilize monthly with quarter-strength fertilizer.

Tips

Vinca is a useful, attractive filler plant for containers and hanging baskets. It is heat tolerant but not able to withstand prolonged cold spells.

Also called: Madagascar periwinkle
Features: mounding to trailing habit; wide range of flower colors; blooms throughout summer; deep green foliage **Height:** 6–18"
Spread: 10–24" **Hardiness:** annual
Grow rating: easy

Recommended

C. hybrida '**First Kiss Blueberry**' has deep lavender blooms with unique violet-blue centers and is an All-America Selections winner.

C. roseus (Madagascar periwinkle) forms compact mounds of spreading branches. NIRVANA CASCADE SERIES is one of the most disease-tolerant vincas. Look for '**Cascade Lavender with Eye,**' '**Cascade White,**' '**Cascade Shell Pink**' and '**Cascade Pink.**' There are also eight upright selections in NIRVANA CASCADE SERIES. **Pacifica Series** is more upright, to 18" tall, with an equal spread. Flowers come in apricot, burgundy, coral, dark red, orchid and pink. '**Sante Fe**' features vibrant salmon flowers with a contrasting white eye on compact, 8" plants. COOLER SERIES has large, 2" blooms with overlapping petals that look like impatiens.

Weigela
Weigela

Some of the most exciting breeding work in horticulture has been done on this shrub to the point where the compact, long-flowering cultivars are a good choice for a specimen container plant.

Growing

Weigelas prefer **full sun** but tolerate partial shade. The potting mix should be **well drained**. Fertilize monthly during the growing season with half-strength fertilizer. Move containers to a sheltered location protected from temperature fluctuations in winter.

Tips

With their attractive foliage and long flowering period, weigelas are great as focal points alone or in mixed containers. Combine a purple-leaved weigela with a silver-leaved, white-flowered, trailing plant such as snow-in-summer to soften the edge of the container and to create contrast.

Recommended

W. florida is a bushy, spreading shrub with arching branches that bears clusters of dark pink flowers. Many hybrids and cultivars are available. CARNAVAL bears red, white or pink flowers. FINE WINE is a compact selection of WINE & ROSES with good branching, dark burgundy foliage and hot pink flowers. MIDNIGHT WINE is a low, mounding dwarf with dark burgundy foliage. 'Polka' has bright pink flowers. 'Red Prince' produces dark red flowers. 'Rubidor' has yellow foliage and red flowers. 'Variegata' has yellow and green variegated foliage and pink flowers. WINE & ROSES bears dark burgundy foliage and rosy pink flowers.

W. florida FINE WINE, a Proven Winners Color Choice Selection

Weigela will become too large for a container after three to five years and should be moved to the garden when it does.

Features: upright or low, spreading, deciduous shrub; attractive, late-spring, early-summer and, sporadically, fall flowers; green, bronze or purple foliage **Height:** 1–6' **Spread:** 1–4' **Hardiness:** zones 3–8 **Grow rating:** easy

Yarrow

Achillea

A. millefolium 'Paprika'

Yarrow cultivars come in a range of colors with deep green, ferny foliage. However you use them, they will endure drought and keep growing. To get repeat blooms, be sure to deadhead.

Features: clump-forming perennial; white, cream, yellow, red, orange, pink, salmon or purple, mid-summer to early-fall flowers; attractive foliage; spreading habit **Height:** 4"–4' **Spread:** 12–36" **Hardiness:** zones 2–8 **Grow rating:** medium

Growing

Yarrows grow best in **full sun**. The potting mix should be **light** and **well drained**. These plants tolerate drought. Fertilize no more than monthly during the growing season with quarter-strength fertilizer. Too much fertilizer results in weak, floppy growth. Deadhead to prolong blooming. In winter, move containers to a sheltered location protected from temperature fluctuations.

Tips

Yarrow thrives in hot, dry locations where nothing else will grow. If you often forget to water, yarrow could be the plant for you. Combine it with other drought-tolerant plants for a colorful, low-maintenance container.

Recommended

A. millefolium (common yarrow) forms a clump of soft, finely divided foliage and bears white flowers. Many cultivars exist, with flowers in a wide range of colors. **'Apple Blossom'** has light pink flowers. **'Paprika'** bears yellow-centered, red flowers that fade to pink, yellow or cream. **'Summer Pastels'** bears white, pink, yellow, purple and sometimes red or salmon-colored flowers. **'Terra Cotta'** has orange-red flowers that fade to light rusty orange or creamy orange.

Yarrow will happily self-seed, eventually turning up in most of your containers and anywhere else the seeds happen to land.

A. millefolium 'Summer Pastels' (above),
A. millefolium (below)

A. millefolium 'Summer Pastels'

Yew

Taxus

T. x media 'Sunburst' (above)
T. x media 'Densiformis' (below)

Yews are among the only reliable evergreens for full sun and deep shade. They are often used to create topiary specimens and can be clipped to maintain a small, neat form for a container.

Growing

Yews grow well in any light conditions from **full sun to full shade**. The potting mix should be **moist** and **well drained**. Fertilize monthly during the growing season with half-strength fertilizer. Move them to a sheltered location out of the wind and sun in winter.

Tips

Specimens can be planted alone or used with annuals and perennials for a mixed display. Male and female flowers are borne on separate plants. Both must be present for the attractive, red arils (seed cups) to form.

Recommended

T. x media (English-Japanese yew), a cross between *T. baccata* (English yew) and *T. cuspidata* (Japanese yew), has the vigor of English yew and the cold hardiness of Japanese yew. It forms a rounded, upright tree or shrub, though the size and form can vary among the many cultivars. **'Brownii'** is a dense, rounded cultivar. **'Hicksii'** is a narrow, columnar form. **'Tautonii'** is a slow-growing, rounded, spreading cultivar.

These trees tolerate windy, dry and polluted conditions but dislike excessive heat, and on the hotter south or southwest side of a building, they may suffer needle scorch.

Features: conical, columnar, bushy or spreading, evergreen tree or shrub; attractive foliage; red fruit **Height:** 1–10'
Spread: 1–5' **Hardiness:** zones 4–7
Grow rating: medium

Yucca

Yucca

Y. filamentosa with maidenhair vine, African daisy, vinca and dracaena

ucca makes an upright, architectural statement in a combination planter, or it can be used as a specimen to give a container a southwestern feel.

Growing

Yucca grows best in **full sun** but tolerates partial shade. The potting mix must be **well drained**. This plant is very drought tolerant. Fertilize no more than once a month during the growing

Yucca fruits rarely develop in the Midwest. The yucca moth, which pollinates the flowers, is uncommon outside the plant's native range.

Also called: Adam's needle **Features:** stiff, rosette-forming, evergreen perennial; white or creamy, summer flowers; stiff, decorative foliage **Height:** 24–36"; up to 6' in flower **Spread:** 24–36" **Hardiness:** zones 5–10 **Grow rating:** medium

season with quarter-strength fertilizer. Flower spikes can be removed when flowering is finished, and dead leaves can be removed as needed. Move it to a sheltered location in winter, or just leave it where it is, enjoy it covered in snow and, if it doesn't make it through winter, simply replace it in spring.

Tips

The upright, narrow leaves have the same effect as spike in the background of a combination planter. Use yucca with low, soft, trailing plants to create contrast.

Recommended

Y. filamentosa has long, stiff, finely serrated, pointed leaves with threads that peel back from the edges. It is the most frost-hardy species available. **'Bright Edge'** has leaves with yellow margins. **'Golden Sword'** has leaves with yellow centers and green margins. **'Hofer's Blue'** has attractive, blue-green leaves and is salt tolerant.

Y. filamentosa (above), Y. filamentosa 'Bright Edge' (below)

Y. filamentosa 'Golden Sword' (below)

Glossary

Acidic soil: soil with a pH lower than 7.0

Annual: a plant that germinates, flowers, sets seed and dies in one growing season

Alkaline soil: soil with a pH higher than 7.0

Basal foliage: leaves that form from the crown, at the base of the plant

Bract: a modified leaf at the base of a flower or flower cluster

Corm: a bulb-like, food-storing, underground stem, resembling a bulb without scales

Crown: the part of the plant at or just below soil level where the shoots join the roots

Cultivar: a cultivated plant variety with one or more distinct differences from the species, e.g., in flower color or disease resistance

Deadhead: to remove spent flowers to maintain a neat appearance and encourage a longer blooming season

Direct sow: to sow seeds directly in the garden

Dormancy: a period of plant inactivity, usually during winter or unfavorable conditions

Double flower: a flower with an unusually large number of petals

Espalier: a tree trained from a young age to grow on a single plane

Genus: a category of biological classification between the species and family levels; the first word in a scientific name indicates the genus

Grafting: a type of propagation in which a stem or bud of one plant is joined onto the rootstock of another plant of a closely related species

Hardy: capable of surviving cold weather or frost without protection

Hip: the fruit of a rose, containing the seeds

Humus: decomposed or decomposing organic material in the soil

Hybrid: a plant resulting from natural or human-induced cross-breeding between varieties, species or genera

Neutral soil: soil with a pH of 7.0

Offset: a horizontal branch that forms at the base of a plant and produces new plants from buds at its tips

Panicle: a compound flower structure with groups of flowers on short stalks

Perennial: a plant that takes three or more years to complete its life cycle

pH: a measure of acidity or alkalinity

Rhizome: a root-like, food-storing stem that grows horizontally at or just below soil level, from which new shoots may emerge

Rootball: the root mass and surrounding soil of a plant

Seedhead: dried, inedible fruit that contains seeds; the fruiting stage of the inflourescence

Self-seeding: reproducing by means of seeds without human assistance, so that new plants constantly replace those that die

Semi-double flower: a flower with petals in two or three rings

Single flower: a flower with a single ring of typically four or five petals

Species: the fundamental unit of biological classification; the entity from which cultivars and varieties are derived

Standard: a shrub or small tree grown with an erect main stem, accomplished either through pruning and training or by grafting the plant onto a tall, straight stock

Sucker: a shoot that comes up from the root, often some distance from the plant; it can be separated to form a new plant once it develops its own roots

Tender: incapable of surviving the climatic conditions of a given region and requiring protection from frost or cold

Tuber: the thick section of a rhizome bearing nodes and buds

Variegation: foliage that has more than one color, often patched or striped or bearing leaf margins of a different color

Variety: a naturally occurring variant of a species

SPECIES
by Common Name

Species	Full Sun	Partial Shade	Light Shade	Full Shade	Moist	Well-drained	Drought-tolerant	Fertile	Average	Low	Thriller	Spiller	Filler
African Daisy	•				•	•		•	•				•
Alternanthera	•				•	•			•			•	•
Arborvitae	•	•	•		•	•			•	•	•		
Asparagus Fern		•	•		•				•			•	•
Bacopa		•			•	•			•			•	
Banana	•				•	•		•			•		
Basil	•				•	•		•	•				•
Begonia		•	•		•	•		•	•		•	•	•
Black-Eyed Susan	•	•			•	•	•		•				•
Black-Eyed Susan Vine	•	•	•		•	•			•			•	
Blood Grass	•	•			•				•		•		•
Blueberry	•				•	•			•	•	•		
Blue Fescue	•	•			•	•	•		•	•	•		•
Caladium		•	•	•	•	•		•	•		•		
Calla Lily	•				•	•			•		•		
Canna Lily	•				•	•			•		•		
Clematis	•				•	•			•		•	•	
Clover	•	•			•	•				•		•	•
Coleus		•	•		•	•		•	•		•		•
Coral Bells		•	•		•	•		•	•				•
Croton	•				•	•		•	•		•		
Cuphea	•	•			•	•			•				•
Dahlia	•				•	•		•	•		•		•
Daylily	•	•	•	•	•	•	•		•		•		•
Diascia	•				•	•		•	•			•	•
Dichondra	•				•	•	•		•			•	
Dusty Miller	•					•			•	•			•
Dwarf Morning Glory	•					•				•		•	•
Elder	•	•			•	•			•	•	•		
Elephant Ears		•	•		•				•		•		
English Ivy		•	•		•	•			•			•	
Euonymus	•				•	•			•	•	•	•	
Euphorbia	•		•		•	•				•	•		•

Upright	Bushy	Clump-forming	Spreading	Climber/Trailer	Groundcover	Flowers	Foliage	Fruit/Seed	Scent	Habit	Page Number	SPECIES by Common Name
•	•		•			•					64	African Daisy
•	•		•				•				65	Alternanthera
•	•						•			•	66	Arborvitae
		•		•			•			•	68	Asparagus Fern
	•		•			•				•	69	Bacopa
•							•	•		•	70	Banana
	•					•	•		•		71	Basil
	•	•		•		•	•				72	Begonia
•		•				•					74	Black-Eyed Susan
				•		•	•			•	76	Black-Eyed Susan Vine
•		•	•				•			•	77	Blood Grass
	•					•	•	•	•		78	Blueberry
•		•					•			•	80	Blue Fescue
•		•					•			•	81	Caladium
•		•				•	•			•	82	Calla Lily
•		•				•	•			•	84	Canna Lily
		•			•	•	•			•	85	Clematis
	•		•			•	•			•	87	Clover
•	•						•			•	88	Coleus
		•	•			•	•				90	Coral Bells
•	•						•			•	92	Croton
•	•					•				•	93	Cuphea
	•	•				•	•			•	94	Dahlia
		•				•	•				96	Daylily
	•		•			•				•	97	Diascia
					•		•			•	98	Dichondra
	•	•					•				99	Dusty Miller
	•		•			•				•	100	Dwarf Morning Glory
•	•					•	•	•		•	101	Elder
		•					•			•	103	Elephant Ears
				•			•			•	105	English Ivy
		•		•			•			•	106	Euonymus
•	•	•				•	•			•	107	Euphorbia

SPECIES by Common Name	LIGHT				MOISTURE			FERTILITY			USE		
	Full Sun	Partial Shade	Light Shade	Full Shade	Moist	Well-drained	Drought-tolerant	Fertile	Average	Low	Thriller	Spiller	Filler
Fan Flower	•		•		•	•			•			•	•
Flowering Maple	•		•		•	•			•		•		•
Fuchsia		•	•		•	•		•	•		•	•	
Geranium	•					•			•			•	•
Golden Hakone Grass		•	•		•	•			•			•	•
Golden Marguerite	•					•	•	•	•	•	•		
Hardy Geranium		•	•						•				
Heliotrope	•				•	•			•				•
Hens and Chicks	•	•				•	•			•			•
Hosta		•	•		•	•			•				•
Hydrangea	•	•			•	•		•	•		•		
Impatiens		•	•		•	•		•	•		•		•
Iris	•				•	•			•		•		
Japanese Painted Fern		•	•	•	•				•				•
Lady's Mantle		•	•		•	•		•	•				•
Lamium		•	•		•	•			•	•		•	•
Lantana	•				•	•	•	•	•		•	•	•
Lavender	•					•	•		•	•			•
Lemon	•					•			•		•		
Licorice Plant	•					•			•			•	
Lobelia	•	•			•	•			•			•	•
Lotus Vine	•	•				•	•		•	•		•	•
Maidenhair Fern		•	•		•	•			•	•			•
Mandevilla	•				•	•		•	•		•	•	
Maple	•		•			•		•	•	•	•		
Maracas Brazilian Fireworks		•	•	•	•	•			•		•		•
Million Bells	•				•	•			•			•	•
Mondo Grass	•		•		•	•		•	•				•
Nasturtium	•				•	•			•	•		•	•
Nemesia	•				•	•			•			•	•
Nicotiana	•	•	•		•	•		•	•		•		
Oregano	•					•			•	•			•
Ornamental Pepper	•				•	•		•	•		•		•

	FORM						FEATURES						SPECIES by Common Name
Upright	Bushy	Clump-forming	Spreading	Climber/Trailer	Groundcover	Flowers	Foliage	Fruit/Seed	Scent	Habit	Page Number	
	•			•		•				•	109	Fan Flower
•	•					•	•			•	110	Flowering Maple
•	•			•		•				•	111	Fuchsia
•	•			•		•	•		•		112	Geranium
		•					•			•	114	Golden Hakone Grass
	•		•			•	•				115	Golden Marguerite
•	•	•				•	•				116	Hardy Geranium
	•					•	•		•	•	118	Heliotrope
					•	•	•			•	119	Hens and Chicks
		•				•	•			•	120	Hosta
	•		•	•		•	•			•	122	Hydrangea
•	•		•			•				•	124	Impatiens
•		•				•	•			•	126	Iris
		•	•				•			•	128	Japanese Painted Fern
	•					•	•				130	Lady's Mantle
			•		•	•	•			•	131	Lamium
	•			•		•	•				133	Lantana
•	•					•	•		•		134	Lavender
•	•					•	•	•	•		135	Lemon
				•			•			•	136	Licorice Plant
•	•			•		•				•	137	Lobelia
	•			•		•	•			•	139	Lotus Vine
		•	•				•			•	140	Maidenhair Fern
				•		•	•			•	141	Mandevilla
•	•						•	•		•	142	Maple
•	•					•	•				144	Maracas Brazilian Fireworks
	•			•		•				•	145	Million Bells
					•	•	•			•	146	Mondo Grass
	•		•	•		•	•		•	•	147	Nasturtium
	•		•	•		•				•	148	Nemesia
•	•					•			•	•	149	Nicotiana
•	•					•	•		•		150	Oregano
•	•							•		•	151	Ornamental Pepper

SPECIES
by Common Name

Species	Full Sun	Partial Shade	Light Shade	Full Shade	Moist	Well-drained	Drought-tolerant	Fertile	Average	Low	Thriller	Spiller	Filler
Oxalis	•	•				•		•	•		•		•
Pansy	•				•	•			•				•
Parsley	•	•			•	•			•				•
Perilla	•	•			•	•		•			•		•
Periwinkle		•	•	•	•	•			•	•		•	
Petunia	•					•			•	•	•	•	•
Phormium	•				•	•			•		•		
Piggyback Plant		•	•	•	•	•			•			•	•
Plectranthus			•	•	•	•			•			•	•
Purple Fountain Grass	•					•			•	•	•		
Rose	•				•	•		•	•		•		
Rosemary	•				•	•			•	•	•	•	•
Rush	•	•			•				•	•	•		
Salvia	•				•	•		•	•		•		
Scarlet Runner Bean	•				•	•			•		•	•	
Sedge	•	•			•				•		•		
Sedum	•					•			•	•			•
Snapdragon	•					•		•	•			•	•
Spider Flower	•				•	•	•		•	•	•		
Spider Plant		•	•		•	•	•		•				•
Spike	•	•			•	•		•	•		•		
Spruce	•				•	•			•	•	•		
Swan River Daisy	•					•			•			•	•
Sweet Alyssum	•					•			•				•
Sweet Flag	•				•				•		•		•
Sweet Potato Vine	•					•			•	•		•	•
Thyme	•					•	•		•	•		•	•
Tropical Hibiscus	•	•	•		•	•		•	•		•		
Verbena	•					•			•			•	•
Vinca	•	•			•	•	•		•	•		•	•
Weigela	•					•			•		•		
Yarrow	•					•	•	•	•				•
Yew	•	•	•	•	•	•			•		•		
Yucca	•					•	•	•	•		•		

Upright	Bushy	Clump-forming	Spreading	Climber/Trailer	Groundcover	Flowers	Foliage	Fruit/Seed	Scent	Habit	Page Number	SPECIES by Common Name
	•		•			•	•			•	152	Oxalis
		•				•					153	Pansy
	•	•					•			•	155	Parsley
	•						•			•	156	Perilla
				•	•	•	•			•	157	Periwinkle
	•		•			•				•	158	Petunia
•							•			•	160	Phormium
	•	•					•			•	161	Piggyback Plant
•			•	•			•			•	162	Plectranthus
		•				•	•			•	163	Purple Fountain Grass
	•					•			•		165	Rose
•	•		•			•	•		•		167	Rosemary
		•					•			•	168	Rush
	•					•	•			•	169	Salvia
				•		•		•		•	171	Scarlet Runner Bean
		•					•			•	172	Sedge
•			•		•	•	•			•	174	Sedum
	•	•				•	•			•	175	Snapdragon
•						•	•			•	176	Spider Flower
		•					•			•	177	Spider Plant
•							•			•	178	Spike
•	•						•			•	179	Spruce
	•		•			•	•			•	180	Swan River Daisy
	•		•			•	•		•	•	181	Sweet Alyssum
		•					•			•	182	Sweet Flag
	•		•	•		•	•			•	183	Sweet Potato Vine
	•				•	•	•		•		185	Thyme
	•					•	•			•	186	Tropical Hibiscus
•	•		•			•				•	187	Verbena
	•		•			•	•			•	188	Vinca
		•				•	•			•	189	Weigela
		•	•			•	•			•	190	Yarrow
•			•				•	•		•	192	Yew
•						•	•			•	193	Yucca

Index of Recommended Plant Names

Main entries are in **boldface**; botanical names are in *italics*.

Flowering Maple

Hosta

Lobelia

Maracas Brazilian Fireworks

Perilla

Rosemary

Salvia

Tradescantia

Weigela

About the Authors

William Aldrich has written about gardening since 1980, mostly for the *Chicago Tribune*. He is an award-winning author of more than 200 articles and is a past president of the Garden Writers Association. A lifelong resident of the Chicago area, he founded *Chicagoland Gardening Magazine* in 1995 and remains its publisher.

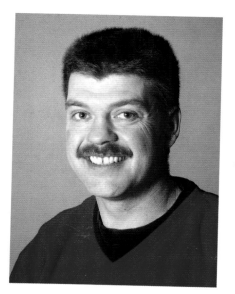

Don Williamson has turned his passion for gardening into his life's work. His background is in landscaping, golf course construction and management, and in the design and construction of formal landscape settings. With a degree in Applied Horticultural Technology and professional certificates in Turf Management, he has written and co-written several gardening books.

Alison Beck has been gardening since she was a child. Author of more than two dozen gardening books, she showcases her talent for practical advice and her passion for gardening. Alison has a diploma in Horticultural Technology and a degree in Creative Writing.

Laura Peters is a certified Master Gardener with experience in every aspect of the horticultural industry. A talented garden photographer whose work is featured in many gardening books, she enjoys sharing her practical knowledge of organic gardening, plant varieties and gardening products with fellow gardeners.

More Great Gardening Guides from Lone Pine Publishing

HERB GARDENING FOR THE MIDWEST
by Debra Knapke and Laura Peters

The herb garden holds special status in the realm of gardening. It is an unbeatable source of fresh flavor for home cooking, of folkloric remedies for common ailments and of delightful beauty for the gardening enthusiast. Herbs encompass a wide range of useful plants: everything from herbaceous perennials to trees, shrubs, vines, lichens and fungi. Herbs may be culinary in use or medicinal. They can flavor soup or act as a natural pesticide. In *Herb Gardening for the Midwest*, the authors profile 90 herbs that can be grown under regional conditions and provide ample information concerning cultivation and care.

Softcover • 240 pages • full color photographs throughout • 8.5" x 5.5"
ISBN 978-976-8200-38-9 • $19.95
Publication Date: April 2008

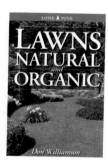

LAWNS NATURAL AND ORGANIC
by Don Williamson

This book is committed to the development of high-quality lawns achieved through natural, chemical-free practices. Turf management expert Don Williamson provides a comprehensive overview of grass types, proper lawn installation, healthy maintenance practices and controlling pests and diseases. States covered by this book include North Dakota, South Dakota, northern Kansas, Nebraska, Minnesota, Wisconsin, Iowa, northern Missouri, Illinois, Indiana, Ohio and Michigan.

Softcover • 160 pages • full color photographs throughout • 8.5" x 5.5"
ISBN 978-976-8200-14-3 • $16.95

BEST GARDEN PLANTS FOR KANSAS • $16.95 • 978-976-8200-32-7

ANNUALS FOR MINNESOTA AND WISCONSIN • $18.95 • 978-1-55105-381-3
BEST GARDEN PLANTS FOR MINNESOTA AND WISCONSIN • $16.95 • 978-1-55105-483-4
TREE AND SHRUB GARDENING FOR MINNESOTA AND WISCONSIN • $18.95 • 978-1-55105-483-4

BEST GARDEN PLANTS FOR IOWA • $15.95 • 978-1-55105-520-6

BEST GARDEN PLANTS FOR MISSOURI • $16.95 • 978-976-8200-12-9

ANNUALS FOR ILLINOIS
BEST GARDEN PLANTS FOR ILLINOIS • $16.95 • 978-1-55105-502-2
GARDENING MONTH BY MONTH IN ILLINOIS • $15.95 • 978-1-55105-375-2
TREE AND SHRUB GARDENING FOR ILLINOIS • $18.95 • 978-1-55105-404-9

ANNUALS FOR MICHIGAN • $18.95 • 978-1-55105-346-2
BEST GARDEN PLANTS FOR MICHIGAN • $15.95 • 978-1-55105-498-8
GARDENING MONTH BY MONTH IN MICHIGAN • $15.95 • 978-1-55105-363-9
ROSES FOR MICHIGAN • $18.95 • 978-1-55105-367-7
TREE AND SHRUB GARDENING FOR MICHIGAN • $18.95 • 978-1-55105-347-9

ANNUALS FOR OHIO • $18.95 • 978-1-55105-388-2
BEST GARDEN PLANTS FOR OHIO • $15.95 • 978-1-55105-496-4
GARDENING MONTH BY MONTH IN OHIO • $15.95 • 978-1-55105-406-3
TREE AND SHRUB GARDENING FOR OHIO • $18.95 • 978-1-55105-402-5

Available at your local bookseller or order direct from Lone Pine Publishing at
1-800-518-3541.

www.lonepinepublishing.com